Thrift in the Household

by

Dora Morrell Hughes

APPLEWOOD BOOKS
Bedford, Massachusetts

Thrift in the Household

was originally published in

1918

ISBN: 978-1-4290-1025-2

Thank you for purchasing an Applewood book. Applewood reprints America's lively classics— books from the past that are still of interest to the modern reader.
For a free copy of
a catalog of our
bestselling
books,
write
to us at:
Applewood Books
Box 365
Bedford, MA 01730
or visit us on the web at:
For cookbooks: foodsville.com
For our complete catalog: awb.com

Prepared for publishing by HP

THRIFT
IN THE HOUSEHOLD

THRIFT IN THE HOUSEHOLD

BY

DORA MORRELL HUGHES

BOSTON
LOTHROP, LEE & SHEPARD CO.

Published, March, 1918

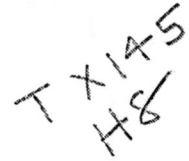

COPYRIGHT, 1918,
BY LOTHROP, LEE & SHEPARD CO.

All Rights Reserved

THRIFT IN THE HOUSEHOLD

Norwood Press
BERWICK & SMITH CO.
NORWOOD, MASS.
U. S. A.

"Annual income twenty pounds, annual expenditure nineteen nineteen six, result happiness. Annual income twenty pounds, annual expenditure twenty pounds ought and six, result misery."

—Mr. Micawber in *"David Copperfield."*

CONTENTS

CHAPTER		PAGE
I.	WHAT THRIFT IS AND IS NOT	9
II.	BUYING	19
III.	MANAGING, AND LITTLE LEAKS	37
IV.	LITTLE ECONOMIES	49
V.	VINEGARS. EGGS	75
VI.	THE GREATEST ECONOMY: YOURSELF	89
VII.	LABOR-SAVING	107
VIII.	BREAD AND CAKE	115
IX.	SOUPS	133
X.	OILS AND FATS	149
XI.	COAL AND ICE	167
XII.	POSSIBILITIES OF CORN MEAL	185
XIII.	MEAT AND MEAT SUBSTITUTES	195
XIV.	DESSERTS	225
XV.	THRIFT AND TEXTILES	243
XVI.	CARE OF CLOTHING	257
XVII.	THE FAMILY GARDEN	277

CHAPTER I
WHAT THRIFT IS AND IS NOT

THRIFT IN THE HOUSEHOLD

CHAPTER I

WHAT THRIFT IS AND IS NOT

THRIFT is the making the best of what one has in strength, time, or money; getting one hundred per cent. in one's relations with life. Thrift is an appreciation and application of the accumulative force of little things. Thrift is a constructive force; waste is its destructive opposite. Sometimes thrift is saving, going without; sometimes thrift is spending—" there is a scattering that increaseth "—but always it is something for something. Thrift is the base on which success of every kind is built, for either thrift or waste is used in everything. The business man applies thrift when he finds the measure by which he can reduce his "overhead" by the fraction of a cent, for he realizes that these fractions soon grow into dollars.

Philosophers, since first there were philosophers, have been telling their hearers that there were no trifles, but the American households as a whole have been managed as if to use no more than was needed, to save the bit here and there, were beneath their dignity. Women know less of thrift and more of an uneven, haphazard effort at saving than is consistent with their duty as partners in home-making; unfortunately, too often they have no respect for nor appreciation of the power that lies in their hands, and therefore fail to realize the possibilities of the material with which they work, and their servants have imitated them, and have despised economy as stinginess, which is quite another matter. Stinginess is selfishness. If you notice, you will find the givers among the thrifty. What they have not wasted they share with others. Every article, however small it may be, that is wasted must be replaced and it is "the little foxes that spoil the vines." Few persons waste dollars at a time, but they waste many in cents. The Woolworth Building, and the Fifth Avenue house, built, as the megaphone man tells his hearers, from five-cent and ten-cent pieces, are object lessons in the financial advantage of saving trifles.

There is no thrift in saving when the value of the article saved is less than the expense of saving it. Sometimes there is more thrift in throwing away than in saving. Does that seem a paradox? Not long since, when eggs were sixty cents a dozen and bread six cents a loaf, there was an article in a home publication on the importance of saving bread crumbs, and as an illustration how to do this a recipe for a bread-pudding was given. This called for a cup of bread crumbs, value less than a cent, and five eggs, cost twenty-five cents, and milk, sugar, and heat. To spend twenty-five cents to save five is waste; to spend twenty-five cents to save thirty is gain. It is not economy to spend time, materials, and strength in making something that the family will not like when it is done.

The average cook, and housekeeper, too, if she has three oranges and is making an orange-pudding which requires two oranges, will use the three. If the housewife objects to using three when two are enough she very likely will hear her cook ask, "What's the use of being so stingy with them? What is one orange good for?" If the housekeeper can tell

WHAT THRIFT IS AND IS NOT 15

her, the cook will appreciate the thrift, otherwise she will continue to waste.

There is an old proverb of our grandmother's day that is equally true to-day though not as often heard: "a woman can throw out with a spoon in the kitchen more than a man can bring in with a shovel." That is because a woman generally does not realize that what she throws out has any money value. There is no more exacting business than housekeeping and home-making. Those wives who think it beneath them and unworthy of their attention simply show their ignorance of what it is. That there are so many who feel time spent in work at home to be time wasted explains in a large part why the cost of living has steadily increased. All waste raises the cost of living. What is wasted must be supplied in some other way. Had women handled the money in past years they would have had a better understanding of the value of things with which they worked. So many women do not have the spending of cash that they do not know what one hundred cents are good for.

If the garbage pail is always full, if the housewife says, "My cake isn't as good as usual. I didn't have good luck with it this time," there is much waste in that household. There is no luck about cooking. Cooking is the combination of care and brains expressed in the arrangement of certain materials. Cooking is a branch of chemistry, and should be followed with equal painstaking. Then, it will be equally effective.

It is very thriftless to cook without recipes unless one has cooked so much that with her experience she has learned to measure by eye and feel. Also, it is thriftless for one who has much cooking to do not to master the principles of cooking that she may become independent of recipes. A good cook knows as soon as she reads a recipe whether or not it is worth cooking; there is a law of proportion and affinity governing the combination of food materials, and the less money you have to spend on food, the more it is to your advantage to know the laws of cooking and how to apply them.

An empty garbage pail is the certain indication of two things: how to buy and how to use what one has bought. Thrift does not put slices of bread, halves of stale loaves, bits of vegetables, cheese, bones, and scraps of meat into the garbage pail. Thrift appreciates that a cold potato represents the amount that potato cost plus the expense for heat to cook it; it knows that a loaf of cake spoiled or bread burned, anything that carelessness has left to become sour or worthless, represents an expenditure of money equivalent to what it will cost to replace and cook it. The woman who leaves dough sticking to her mixing-pan will lose considerable bread before the year is done, and she will lose it not merely in that one channel but in others, for one is careless in many things if she is in one.

A very small leak in a ship if left unheeded will sink a good-sized vessel; so the happiness of many a household is wrecked on small things. There can be no real happiness in a home where the outgo is the same as the income or greater, and wherever that is the case there are leakages in the kitchen. It is absolutely impossible for a man to get ahead financially if there is not good management in the kitchen, and good management means taking heed of trifles. The direction that Christ gave His people, "Gather up the fragments that remain, that nothing be lost," has a practical merit to-day.

CHAPTER II
BUYING

CHAPTER II

BUYING

THERE are two avenues through which thrift is cultivated: buying and managing. Usually one is advised to buy in quantity, and if one has storage room, that reduces the cost of articles considerably. Large families serve thrift by buying in quantity, but small families living in flats may find quantity-buying very wasteful. For a large family to buy flour by the bag is as foolish as for a small family to buy it by the barrel. There is more loss proportionately to flour in the bag because it sifts through the holder, but for the small family the loss is smaller than it would be to have a barrel of flour which before it could be eaten would become musty, possibly wormy, unless there were unusual facilities for keeping it.

Cereals and meals, which are only other forms of a cereal, do not keep long unless in a thoroughly dry atmosphere and therefore should be bought in such quantity that they will be eaten before must or insects corrupt. Even rice and the so-called sterilized grains will become wormy if kept by the month before using. Canned goods are wisely purchased by the dozen or the case. Of most, the case contains four dozen jars. There is a reduction by the dozen usually, though since prices have become so high many dealers will not sell by the dozen or case. They prefer to retail the cans getting the larger price for them. If you get a reduction of only a cent on a can there is a considerable saving when you think of all the canned fruits and vegetables that go to satisfy the appetite of the ordinary family. Remember the words of Poor

Richard, "Take care of the pennies, and the dollars will take care of themselves."

I believe it is wiser to buy regularly at the same stores than to wander about looking for bargains. Very often so-called bargains have short weight or other weaknesses. Every store has occasional bargains, not always advertised, sales of special values; in the better stores it is to the regular customers that knowledge of these is given, because there never is enough of the stock on sale to be offered for general buying.

Prices are lower in the stores that insist on cash sales and do not deliver goods. It is proper they should be lower, for the expenses of such stores are greatly reduced below those where deliveries are made of every little order any time of day, and cash in hand enables a merchant to buy more cheaply and so to sell at better advantage to the buyer. These cash stores save the salaries of bookkeepers made necessary by charge accounts, and they are also free from losses from uncollectible bills.

When men are buyers they watch the printed list of prices and conditions of what they will buy; when women are buyers they often go to their buying without knowing anything about the standard price and variations from that. They do not know whether articles are plenty and cheap or scarce and high. Men know what they should be charged for what they buy; women often buy without asking the price of what they are getting.

In every city of any size a market price list is printed once or twice a week giving prices and market conditions of foods. The home member of the matrimonial partnership should study these lists. Even if she pays as much she will know more what she gets. The buyer should

BUYING

know if she is getting sixteen ounces to the pound.

A scale for the kitchen running as high as twenty-five pounds is almost as great a necessity as a dishpan. If you pay nine and a half cents a pound for sugar and get fifteen ounces only instead of a full pound you will pay for many pounds of sugar that you never get. Perhaps you lack the moral courage to exact of your dealer what belongs to you. Remember that any one who is willing to be robbed will always find the thief to rob her.

It is possible to avoid any unpleasantness in securing your dues by saying to a grocer with whom you begin trading, "I see that your measures are full and generous to your customers. I always weigh my packages and it is a satisfaction to know that you are as just to me as to yourself." Thus you accomplish three things: you show that you are " on your job," that you are watching how things go, and you tell him this by praise, which is better than finding fault.

If a package is short-weight and you wish to continue to trade there you can say, " I would like to have you see to this yourself as last time your clerk was careless with his weighing." If you have no grounds for praise you should take your business elsewhere, and not help a man to success in thievery, for he is as truly a thief who takes an ounce from your pound as he is who takes the money for it from your pocket.

Another great waste for the consumer has developed from what is said to be a commendable measure, that is, the fancy box and carton business. This is claimed to be more sanitary, and so it is in a few instances, but as a whole it is a claim unjustified by facts, and a decided item in increasing the cost of living. In some instances it more than doubles the cost of the article contained. It is sanitary to wrap bread, cakes, pies, crackers, and articles to be eaten without further cooking, but what good is served by placing in close cartons such foods as rice, and those things which must be cooked before serving? All cereals are thoroughly cooked after being taken from cartons and are thus sterilized. Why pay double for them? Corn meal sold in cartons costs nearly three times as much as that bought in bulk. It keeps no better, tastes no better, and must go through the same processes for cooking as that bought by the pound. The same is true of other things.

The first package I ate of seeded raisins stated on the wrapper that they were cleaned, and being of a naturally trusting nature I used the raisins in a cake without washing. The cake was spoiled. From a cupful of raisins, sold in cartons because of cleanliness, I have found a saltspoonful of sand, beside stalks. The cook who does not wash her raisins will have regrets and a few other things. Then, why not buy raisins by the pound rate open? The same is true of dried fruits and many other articles. They all have to be as carefully looked over, washed, and treated as if they had not been placed in cartons as a sanitary measure for cleanliness. There is a good deal of humbug about the extra cleanliness of things packed in special containers, but there is no doubt that some things are better thus treated and that more are not. Employ containers for cooked foods, omit them for foods to be cooked, and thus encourage thrift.

Whether it is thrift to make all dealings on a cash basis or to run accounts is a mooted question with something to be said on both sides and the weight in favor of cash payments. Running bills usually leads to spending more; it is so easy to say, "Charge it," when you see something tempting that you would not buy if you were paying cash for everything. Persons who spend recklessly by instinct should never run bills—they will find the entire income mortgaged before it is due. Those who calculate all expenses of the household and have will enough to hold by their calculations have the use of their money thirty days longer, and of credit in an emergency, for it is one of the peculiarities of the business world that it is easier for a man to get credit who is slack about paying for what he buys than for a man who has always followed the Biblical injunction to "owe no man anything." If such a one asks time it is at once taken for granted that conditions are unfavorable with him and that he will be a risk to the merchant.

The average consumer will save ten per cent. by living on a cash basis and have the satisfaction of knowing what money she has is hers. The apostle of thrift will favor living on a cash basis and making the most of what one has. If the housewife is allowed only five dollars weekly for her table she must plan so carefully that she has at least a dime left with which to build a reserve fund. Thrift lies in small savings. Unless she saves her little she can never become a thrifty buyer. It is always possible to save something if one does not despise the day of small things. It may not be possible to save a quarter though it will be to save a nickel or dime. Thrift makes the housewife plan according to her income, not according to her desires. No one claims that a table can be as well furnished or as much can be done with five dollars as with three times that amount, but the skill of the housewife and the mistress of thrift is never better employed than in making her wits do the most that can be done with what she has.

Until one tries to do it she has no idea how interesting she can find the accomplishing of this aim. To the doer the promise holds true: "Thou hast been faithful over a few things, I will make thee a ruler over many things."

There is a mistaken idea of thrift which sometimes influences the would-be economist to buy articles by their cost price alone, without reflecting whether the lower price gives proper value for what is bought, whether it has as much proportionately of material as the higher priced. It is not what you pay that makes the important factor in living but what *you get* for what you pay. For instance: here are two baskets of apples; the fruit in one is large and speckless, that of the other is windfalls, bruised, gnarly, and the second is one-third less in price than the first. The second will prove the dearer because it has so large an amount of waste; the first has almost no waste, for the skins are so smooth and fine that from them and the cores may be made several glasses of jelly. From the second basket will be no such profit. In consumption of time for preparation twice as much will be necessary.

A good housewife who never bought poor supplies once said to a critic of her methods, "Only rich people can afford to buy poor stuff, since they do not suffer if a few dollars are thrown away in waste."

The boarding-house keeper who bought two seven-pound turkeys instead of one large bird was not thrifty. The larger birds are a trifle less in cost per pound, the intestinal waste of the larger bird and the skeleton is less than of two smaller birds and the meat is richer. How do I know about the waste of the two? I weighed the waste when I was buying to know how much was thrown away. The larger birds have more meat in proportion to skeleton. It costs more in time to prepare two birds than one. In every respect the large bird is the more thrifty purchase for a large family than the same weight of birds in two bodies.

The foundation of true thrift is getting the proportion of most for the expenditure, not the price. One does not learn this relation all at once or by accident, but by computation. Once learned you may build on it your home of thrift. "There is that scattereth, and yet increaseth, and there is that withholdeth more than is meet, but it tendeth to poverty." The knowledge of this and the ability to use the knowledge are thrift.

This principle explains why of two cuts of meat at the same price one is extravagant and the other is not. It is not alone the cost of porterhouse that makes it inadvisable for one of small means, but the proportion of waste in bone and fat for which one pays. You must always remember you are paying for all this waste at the same price you are paying for the delicious meat.

Never buy second-class canned goods but those you have tested and know to be reliable. At times there are sales of these to make way for the new and then it is good buying to get what you need. Good cans have ends slightly concaved and if dented will remain so. Twice-soldered cans are not to be recommended.

Keep all articles in tin, earthenware, or glass, although no acids nor liquids should be kept in tin. Have containers lettered so that you do not handle more than the one wanted when you go for anything, and keep the covers on them when not being used.

Nearly all kitchen supplies may well be bought in quantity, as most of them improve with keeping. Polishes, starch, blueing, all kinds of soap, cleansing-powder, clothes-pins, and such things, are cheaper a year's supply at a time.

BUYING

Sugar keeps indefinitely and should the price ever lower it will be decidedly thrifty to lay in a supply. Never keep sugar—or anything else—in a damp storeroom. It is also far from thrifty for any family to live in a damp house, too damp to store supplies, since it induces disease, and disease is a very heavy expense. Sickness soon reduces any surplus, so that anything which induces depleted strength, whether it be feeding, dressing, thinking, is extravagant. One of the thriftiest habits is that of making the sun welcome in home and self. The best germ-killer is God's own, the sunshine.

Let us sum up the matter of buying thus: Pay cash for everything, or settle all bills at end of a definite time, by week or month.

Examine all supplies as they come in, having a sales order slip by which to check them, and to insure their being of quality and amount ordered. Put them away in their containers as soon as checked.

See that your maid is as careful in use of goods bought in quantity as if they were bought by the pound, and train yourself to the same care if you do your own work. Sugar and flour require special care to save waste as you take from the bins.

Buy when things are in season, not when they are dearest, which is when they are out of season. Buy fruits and vegetables for canning when and where they are most abundant. That is when they are cheapest, and also the best. Things out of season are seldom as good as when their proper time for being eaten has come.

CHAPTER III

MANAGING, AND LITTLE LEAKS

CHAPTER III

MANAGING, AND LITTLE LEAKS

MANAGING is the art and science of using to the best advantage what has been brought into the house. There is no part of the household economy where it is not called upon, no part which is not the better for what New England means when it says of a housekeeper: "She has faculty." Solomon knew her in his time and she to-day is the woman who "looketh well to the ways of her household." It is interesting to notice how like the twentieth-century manager is to this old-time woman in essentials, though conditions have changed so greatly. Read the last chapter of Proverbs and learn what she was and is.

Managing means the charge of waste as well as the first use of everything. It is in the department of management that the wreck of the home happiness comes and financial anxiety with an incompetent manager. A good manager keeps things comfortable. Her mind is easy and therefore she produces ease. She needs no advice but gives it to those who cannot manage time, duties, or money successfully.

System is the secret of good management, and it extends to the smallest detail of home affairs. It softens greatly the jolts of difficult experiences.

She who has learned to prevent little leaks in the home has learned how to make the dollars count for one hundred cents. So many of them are there that one might fill a large book with a list of them. One great mistake for the would-be devotee of thrift is to cook too much at once. Monotony in diet spoils the appetite, the digestion, and wastes the food cooked, for it is refused. Sometimes it is well to cook in large quantities, for many things need hours for their cooking, and it is as cheap to cook much as only what will be used at a single time. The extra quantity may be canned and saved until wanted. For instance, it takes no more fuel to cook three pounds of prunes than to cook half a pound, so I always cook the three pounds and can all but enough for two meals. As my family is small it is more convenient to can often. I fill a jar or more as I have material, set it in the bottom part of the steamer when I am cooking dinner and the same heat sterilizes it that cooks something else. Excess meats, soups, vegetables, and even oatmeal may be saved in this way until one wants it. It is thrift to preserve food thus and the amount quickly accumulates. In our family we dislike to see the same dish served twice in succession, and as we consider waste wicked we avoid it by canning.

The folly of cooking too much for one or two servings lies with those who have not learned what to do with the extra amount. I once saw ten cold potatoes in the garbage pail of a friend whose whole married life had been a struggle with debt. " Why don't you use your potatoes in some other way, in salad, croquettes, baked with cheese or onions, or fried ? " " My family don't like them fixed up in any of those ways." Would not the economic consideration of that fact have led to cooking just enough for the one meal ? It is poor planning that leaves ten good potatoes to be wasted. Do you know there are over three hundred ways in which potatoes may be prepared ?

A skillful manager will overbalance the weakness of a poor buyer, but no buyer can cover the defects of a poor manager. It is the little wastes that destroy the family's peace of mind, though they may not average a farthing's worth each but they are so many they amount to pounds when a year is done. They are to the house what nail-holes would be to a ship if thousands were in the hull. In no department of the unthrifty is there freedom from small wastes. They increase the gas and coal bills, help the plumber to get rich by stopping up the pipes, fill the garbage pail, and so on ad infinitum. Let us consider some of the little wastes.

Soap lies soaking in dish or laundry water. Green soap is used instead of old. Bits of soap are thrown away. Dish-towels are taken for holders and burned. Gas ranges are left lighted when no cooking is going on, or gas is left going full head when a dim light would serve as well. In homes that use stoves instead of gas ranges cords of wood in the shape of boxes are thrown out, yet it all has heating possibilities. Rags and papers are thrown out and so scarce has such material become that the price of paper has risen high enough to bring failure to many publications. I have a friend who saved his newspapers and started his son's college fund by a sale of those saved in a short time. They brought eight dollars, and the price was lower than it has since been. When the three-year-old has become of college age the practice of that kind of thrift will have amounted to considerable.

In the kitchen waste runs riot, often when the housekeeper is her own maid. Cheese is kept in a damp place and becomes covered with a white mould; bits of it that are dried are thrown out; ends, crumbs, and bits of bread accumulate in the garbage pail; a cup of peas or beans, a spoonful of this or that vegetable, bones and scraps from roasts and chops, leftover gravies, all go with the bread. All

MANAGING, AND LITTLE LEAKS 45

of these have possibilities of usefulness and are just that much money wasted.

Milk and cream sour for lack of attention and as soon as sour are turned out. Fruit juices are turned down the sink. Potatoes are pared so generously that more goes with the peeling than into the pot. Bacon fat is turned down the sink, thus disposing of one of the best and most useful fats by stopping up the drainpipe.

Cold potatoes and other vegetables are left to sour; dried fruits and cereals become wormy for want of attention; food is left in tin, which induces unwholesome changes in it; all kinds of winter vegetables and apples are left to sprout and decay for want of picking over.

Boxes of tea, coffee, and spices are left open and the flavor of each is gone; sometimes these things are kept in paper bags, which is worse yet; sugar, tea, coffee, rice, and flour are spilled and wasted in handling; brooms and mops are worn out by being set on the floor. They should be hung.

Tin dishes are not properly dried or are melted by being set on the stove to dry. Tin is less thriftful to buy than enamel, agate, or aluminum. The difference in cost is more than saved in the wear of the dishes. More coal is burned than needed by not closing dampers when fire is not used.

New brooms are used for scrubbing and sweeping paths. Silver spoons are taken for scraping kettles. Sometimes they disappear in the garbage. Steel knives lose their handles from being soaked in hot water. Mustard is left to dry in the pot; pork spoils for want of salt, and beef brine needs scalding. Pickles and olives spoil for want of vinegar or fresh brine. Woodenware is left unscalded and warps, or it splits from being dried in a hot place. Ammonia, gasoline, and other

MANAGING, AND LITTLE LEAKS 47

volatile substances are left loosely corked and evaporate.

Clothes are washed with strong washing-powder or chloride of lime, lye, or soda and come out rotted and faded. Clothes in one washing have been perforated with tiny holes from chloride-of-lime washing-powder.

There are little wastes at the table as, for instance, putting so much sugar in your cup that it does not dissolve. That means sugar enough for another cup. Another decided waste is too large helpings, which is not to be changed into not giving enough to eat, but it is wiser, if one would save, to help twice than to put too much on one's plate at first.

The butter cut in small blocks or made in shapes and served on the bread and butter plate is to be advised for thrift. Of course you do not throw away butter. On the plate it is perfectly clean even if left, because the knife used for it is used only for that. Let the serving be small but repeated.

Avoid the waste that comes from neglect of your tools. Never let the egg-beater soak, which draws oil from the gears, but wash it at once and set to dry. Care of one's tools doubles their usefulness.

CHAPTER IV
LITTLE ECONOMIES

CHAPTER IV

LITTLE ECONOMIES

THERE need be no waste in the home, for much that seems necessary now may be eliminated and what you have you can turn to some use. In the matter of garbage, which is the largest evident waste, there may be something helpful, particularly for one who has hens or a garden. When garbage is nothing but the leavings made in preparing food for cooking it is proper food for poultry, and if one has a garden it makes good fertilizer. For this it is planted in quite a deep hole. The earth is thrown over it, then more garbage added with perhaps a little lime if the land needs it. Garbage may be placed over the oven of the coal range, and contrary to what you may believe, the heat of the fire will burn it without any odor if the damper is left a little open. It will not injure the stove nor cool the oven. These ashes are a fine dressing for garden or for house-plants.

Potato peelings are strong in carbon and if dried may be used as kindlings, but the truly thrifty housewife cooks her potatoes in their jackets, at least until they can be peeled, which keeps her fingers from being discolored and saves a quarter of an hour or more in the oven. After the peelings can be removed only skin thick the potato may be finished in oven or pot. Potatoes thus peeled, then greased very lightly all over and baked in a hot oven are as nice as baked potatoes can be, and what is better?

Baking potatoes takes considerable gas and every moment of the firing means money spent. You can lessen the time by boiling the potatoes for fifteen or twenty minutes and finishing them in a hot oven. They will be equally good.

If you dislike to peel potatoes you can boil them until nearly done, then peel and continue the cooking. Thus you save the wastage that peeling brings. The best of the potato lies near the skin.

Old potatoes are much improved by being soaked for an hour or more in cold water, then plunged into boiling salted water. Instead of peeling them, remove an inch of the skin all around. All vegetables not directly from the garden are better for being freshened by standing a while in cold water.

When you bake potatoes have the skins dry. Wet potatoes lower the heat of the oven, and as potatoes are largely starch they need the stronger heat to make them light. The heat should do to the starch grains of the potato what it does to the corn that is set to pop over the coals.

Use the little bits of potatoes that are too small for the table by boiling, mashing, and adding to the dough for bread or doughnuts. The proportion is two-fifths as much potato as flour. Many cooks will tell you that bread with the addition of potato is the best bread that can be made. These small potatoes are as good as any for frying, croquettes, or mashing, and though it is tiresome to prepare them it is as good a way of saving money or earning it as any other. "A penny saved is a penny earned." There are a hundred calls for each cent that you save, and the need of them dignifies your saving of the pennies by using little things and wasting nothing.

When you prepare asparagus, instead of throwing away the bottom part that you break off, peel it until you come to the juicy center. Cut it in inch pieces, and put it to cook half an hour earlier than you do the better part of the stalks.

Do not salt until nearly done. You will find what was once waste will be edible and tender. Save the water in which you cook these bits as well as the asparagus proper; the next day add milk, thicken if you prefer, season, and have asparagus soup. Use it as the first course of a dinner.

Instead of buying parsley week after week, why not buy a pot of it? It is ornamental and grows nicely in any sunny window and may be grown in winter in a box in the cellar by a window if it has the sunlight. Parsley is hard to start, but after it has been potted it grows well. One may also grow a pot of thyme, which is pretty enough to grow for its own sake did it lack the merit of being one of the best of seasonings. Crush a leaf between finger and thumb and the room will be fresh with its fragrance. Chives also may be added to the family garden, and with them basil and marjoram. A window-box will provide such a garden for all the year, and these living plants will at most trifling cost furnish seasonings for many kinds of food and additions to salads, to make them different and delightful. The leaves may be gathered occasionally, slowly dried and ground for seasoning. For the out-of-door garden tarragon should be planted. Added to cider vinegar it becomes the delicious tarragon vinegar so much liked for salads.

Tomatoes originally were grown as house-plants. Our grandmothers raised them in pots for their beauty, without so much as a dream that one day they would be eaten more than any other vegetable except potatoes. Then they were "love apples," and held to be deadly to the eater. Is there any reason why she who would have delicacies in winter may not grow her tomatoes in a sunny window as they were grown for years?

The dwarf varieties can be grown in pots nicely. Such plants have thriven in the window of a fireless attic where the sun came for the greater part of the day, but tomatoes or any of these plants will do badly if subjected to coal or illuminating gas. They can endure considerable cold if helped by the sun, but no gas.

One of the greatest economies for the cook who uses a gas range is the set of steamers in which she may cook several things at once. If you would be a thrifty housewife, provide yourself with one of these. In six months you will have about saved its cost in your gas bill. With a set of steamers you can prepare an entire-dinner without having the odor of one thing at all affect the foods above it. Do not buy one of tin, however cheaply it is offered. This is a lesson of experience. I bought "a bargain." It cost forty-nine cents and lasted three weeks. A good one will last for years.

Another great economy that means great saving in fuel and in time, perhaps in unspoiled food, is a fireless cooker. You can have one; if you cannot afford to buy a really good commercial cooker you can make one yourself. I made mine and did well with it. Any receptacle made so air-tight that the cold cannot get in will keep the heat from getting out. Take a box, line it with several layers of newspapers either pasted or tacked on. Nearly fill it with hay or sawdust or crumpled paper. Leave spaces where you will set your kettles. Pack the filling as tight as you can around them, so tight that the hole is left when you take the kettle out. I used mine by starting the food cooking in a tin that would fit into one a little larger. In the second I placed the food receptacle with the boiling food, and filled the second with boiling water. Then this was set into a kettle big enough to hold it and more boiling water. When all were boiling hot they went into the box, each being covered closely, and were covered thickly with the same stuff as the remainder of the box packing. Thus prepared, the food could be left to care for itself. This is an excellent way of cooking tough fowl or meat. Cereals or fruits set to cooking like this when you go to bed will be ready for breakfast the next morning. Nothing ever spoils by over-cooking, and much more time must be allowed for preparing a meal with any fireless cooking. The home-made will do less than the best sold but it will do much more than none at all.

The results obtained in flavor with a fireless are much the same as those obtained by casserole cooking in a hot oven; in each case the juices and flavors are retained instead of dissipated as by ordinary methods. A tightly covered earthen bean-pot is a true casserole, and may be used for the same dishes with much satisfaction, though not as fitting to set upon the table.

Corn cooked on the cob should not be wasted. The grains may be taken from the cob by running the edge of a sharp knife between the rows, not cutting, and these grains are to be spread in a thin layer on a bake sheet and dried thoroughly in a warm oven. When dry, place in close receptacle and keep in cool, dark, dry place. The dark can be secured by wrapping thick brown paper around the receptacle. To use this corn, soak it overnight previously. Many persons like this better than the canned. It may be used for soups, corn pudding, fritters, or any other purpose for which the fresh or canned corn serves. The corn on one cob will make corn custard or fritters for two.

Bits of soap which accumulate, either

in kitchen or in chambers, may serve another term by being set to boil with a little hot water and allowed to cool in a flat dish after all have become soft and united into one mass. Then from the piece may be cut small cakes to be wrapped in pretty paper and appear in the bathroom. For the kitchen, let the soap be left in a jelly, which is a very convenient shape for it to be in when one has scrubbing or laundry to be done.

Use your sour milk with soda for gingerbread, biscuits, griddle-cakes, and such things and you will have lighter results than when you used only sweet milk. If you are afraid of getting too much soda, use with it a like measure of cream of tartar. Some cooks use a spoonful of baking-powder to the spoonful of soda and then the bread or cake never tastes of soda or has a golden glow that is not wanted. Sour cream is very good in salad-dressing. If there is considerable sour milk it can be converted into cottage-cheese by pouring over it boiling water until it is cooked, draining, and dressing with a little butter or cream and salt.

In cooking rhubarb or cranberry sauce, boil until nearly done, add a pinch of soda, and sweeten to taste. The soda neutralizes the acid and about half as much sugar will be enough. Too much soda will make the rhubarb tasteless. Combine rhubarb with strawberries if you have some that seem not quite good enough to be served raw. The flavors combined are delicious.

Oiled surfaces, whether floor or linoleum, should not be wiped with soap and water. Wipe with a cloth wet with kerosene. Do not use ammonia on polished or oiled surfaces or on any surface that you do not want cleaned from its finish.

Cook fruits slowly to bring out their sweetness. This makes prunes much sweeter, and makes it unnecessary to sweeten prunes.

Fabrics soaked in borax water will come out clean with neither cloth nor color injured. Borax water does not harm the hands as harsher cleansers do.

Use everything left over. Bits of meat and even a spoonful of gravy will help to make something or to flavor it, and a spoonful of jelly or jam adds to the pudding-sauce just the touch it needed.

Has your hot-water bottle a leak? If it is from a broken spot in the rubber mend it with layers of mending-tissue larger than the hole. Place a piece of tissue, hold it on with a warm iron, and continue until four or five have been set. Let it cool and harden for a day or more before using. If it leaks around the stopper it needs a new washer. One can be put in place and the bag will last a long time. Do not be in haste to cast anything aside.

As a hint in regard to what you can do with two or three left-overs try this. Perhaps you have two or three potatoes, a tablespoonful of onion. Do you think there is nothing to be done with them? Brown the onion in whatever fat you have, the cheapest being a slice of fat pork cut in small pieces and tried out. Leave these crisp pieces in the pan. After the onion has browned a little, add the potatoes cut in dice. Just before serving stir in a cupful of milk in which you have beaten two eggs. It is a good supper dish.

You can vary this by adding to it minced green pepper, or a little corn, or lima beans. You can use beans, onions, tomatoes, and peppers with or without potatoes in almost any proportion, taking what you have and omitting what you have not. You can be reasonably certain of having something to taste good by such combinations either for hot dishes or for salads. The one rule in making a left-over into something is to be sure it tastes good. No chef can do more.

Lettuce will keep a week fresh and crisp if placed in a cloth or paper bag and then in a tight pail. Keep it in a cool place.

Orange, lemon, and grapefruit peel can be saved, cut in strips, left standing in salted water overnight. In the morning parboil in one or more waters to draw out the bitterness, of which with grapefruit there is considerable, though with orange and lemon only little. Then boil in a thick syrup. Place hot in jars and seal. With boiled rice, it is excellent for dessert; it furnishes another dessert with syrup and toasted crackers; and it may be used like citron. It is also good to eat like candy. Baskets of candied peel make an attractive Christmas or birthday gift.

If you have a chop or steak left that has been cooked, do not think you must discard it because it dries when one tries to warm it. Put it in a covered dish in a steamer and let it heat by steam. The steam does not dry it as oven or pan heat does, and the meat will show little difference from newly cooked meat unless the cover was not tight and the steam ran into the plate as water. Steaming is a much better method of reheating than the one more commonly used.

Do you throw away the green stalks of celery and the leaves and then do you buy celery seed or ground celery for seasoning? That is contrary to thrift. All the leaves and stalks not good for the table may be washed and those which are fit for it cut in dice for salad, and sometimes the outer stalks are excellent when boiled and then dressed with a white sauce. All leaves and stalks not otherwise good should be dried in a slow oven or in the sunshine and then run through the finest of the meat-grinders. It is the best celery seasoning and costs nothing. Keep in tightly closed jars. Keep every kind of seasoning in a close receptacle. All the smell that creeps out is that much of the strength of the seasoning being lost.

Tea and coffee left uncovered soon lose their strength. The best way to buy coffee is in the green berry and in large quantities, as in the green berry it improves by keeping. To get the full aroma and deliciousness of coffee roast and grind it just before making. Use left-over coffee for mixing gingerbread or for gelatine desserts. Never warm it up for a beverage, as the flavor of coffee lies in a volatile oil which soon goes after the coffee is made.

Keep a little bag of mustard and horse-radish in the mouth of a pickle jar and the contents will not mould. If preserves or pickles show signs of mould, remove the mould and cook up again. Mould is not a sign of fermentation, and unless it is shaken through the jar will not harm preserves. Old ladies sometimes say of preserves, " They are sure to be good for there is mould on the top." Unsealed pickles made without mustard and horseradish often are improved by reheating.

If you have made a cake and it fell, keep it and next day steam to serve as pudding, with a good sauce. Usually it comes out very good because it fell from not having baked enough. If cake falls from having had too little flour mixed with it, break it up and soften it with milk or water, as little as possible, then add flour to make a stiff dough with baking-powder in the usual proportion to the amount of flour you add. One mixing-cup of flour is half a pint. Steam or bake, allowing twice as long for steaming as for baking. Never lift the lid of the steamer while cooking cake, dumplings, or puddings. They will fall. If water boils away, add boiling water at one side of the water receptacle.

It is true thrift to make and bake without chance of imperfect result, and this is simply a matter of care and attention to details of mixing and baking. If one has been careless she does well to make amends as directed above. It is also far more profitable to cook only what one needs and to cook that well than to have left-overs and food to be worked up for a second appearance. Practice the thrift that plans according to this principle, but become as expert as possible on using left-over articles of food because there will always be some of them. If you want to know what your thrift amounts to in dollars and cents, try putting in a penny bank whatever is represented by the food you do not waste. You will thus get a realizing sense what thrift means. You will not have gone without any of the foods you wanted, but you will have made them of greater value to the family treasury. Your kitchen scale will tell you how many ounces of meat or other substance goes to your soup, salad, pie, or whatever you make for your economy. It becomes very interesting to learn the practical cash saving by such economy, and this method brings realization. It will surprise you. Your loaf of bread cuts a certain number of slices, the whole being priced at six or twelve cents at present time. How much do you waste when you throw into the garbage one of the slices, or how many fragments does it need to make a third of a loaf?

The next time there is melted ice-cream left don't say, "You may as well throw that out; it isn't any good now." Set it with gelatine for blanc-mange, or thicken it with corn-starch or tapioca for pudding. Two eggs to a pint of liquid stirred in and cooked, makes it a good custard. You can use the left-over cocoa or chocolate in the same way, or you may use it for the liquid in place of milk or water.

You can often use water in mixing a cake instead of milk and the cake will be lighter and less liable to scorch. Dishes containing milk or molasses will scorch readily. Grease well the dishes in which such cakes and pudding are baked, as they stick more than sugar-made articles, and when you lose in that way your profit is less.

Save gas in the range by turning off when not in use if only for two minutes. Matches are cheaper than gas. Do not light until wanted, and turn off five minutes before removing kettle from range. The water will continue to boil for some minutes after the gas is out. In using the gas oven, get the full heat and then turn out the gas for baking articles needing a slight heat. Watch the oven, and when more heat becomes necessary light it again. Most housewives use twice as much gas for the oven as is necessary. An outside lining of sheet asbestos makes the oven hold heat considerably longer.

Lemons, cranberries, and rhubarb may be kept a long time if covered with cold water and sealed. Cut rhubarb in inch pieces, pack in jars, let the cold water from the faucet run on it until it has no bubbles, then seal. Keep in the dark, and it will remain good indefinitely and can be used like the fresh plant. The same method holds good with cranberries. Lemons need the water renewed, and will not keep as well as the others. When they are cheap, squeeze out the juice and mix it half and half with sugar until a jar is filled. Seal. It is ready for use in any way that one wants lemon-juice. A spoonful to a glass makes an excellent lemonade, and for lemon pie it is as good as the fresh lemon. This mixture keeps better than the lemons.

Grate the yellow rind into pure grain alcohol and let it stand. Add a crystal of citric acid. You will have an excellent extract for flavoring. Use only enough alcohol to absorb the oil of the lemon. Dilute for using. I make orange, ginger, and vanilla in the same way. Ginger-root is the slowest to make a strong extract but it makes a better extract than one buys, because it is stronger and costs less. This principle is that on which most extracts are made. You must not use wood alcohol, or denatured alcohol. They are unsafe.

CHAPTER V
VINEGARS. EGGS

CHAPTER V

VINEGARS. EGGS

MAKE your own vinegar. Keep your cider until it turns to vinegar or add to the cider vinegar which you have the old cider, and fruit juices you will not put into pudding sauces or other things. The vinegar into which you turn your liquids must have plenty of "mother" for the starter. Add the water in which you boiled apple peelings not to be made into jelly. Clean potato water may be added. Nothing should be hot when turned into the vinegar, as heat destroys the active principle in the mother. If warm it will the sooner begin to work. Keep in a warm place until fermentation has ceased, clarify if necessary, and strain the vinegar if it does not seem clear. If the made vinegar does not clear readily add to it a half-pint of sweet milk to a gallon of vinegar. It will curdle and settle, taking with it the impurities, after which it may be bottled. The sediment will be the working part of a new vinegar. To destroy the mother, boil it.

Starting with this vinegar you can make fancy vinegars for your use or to give your friends. The general rule for making flavored vinegars is to pour the hot acid on the leaves or whatever is the base of the new vinegar, and leave the two to stand undisturbed from two weeks to a month. Fresh leaves are better than dried but not as easy to get. Any druggist has the dried tarragon, mint, or other herb, but the growing plants are not often seen. Onions, horseradish, mustard, and celery, as well as herbs may be treated with the hot vinegar. Mustard and celery seed will be better if boiled with the vinegar. Fancy vinegars sell at fancy prices and cannot often be bought at that.

Last fall I made a very unusual and good vinegar from the red part of watermelon. The *modus operandi* was mashing the melon, the pulp and juice turned into closed receptacles where it could ferment. All vinegars when making must have heat and be kept warm with the sun if not otherwise. The watermelon juice cleared itself, and when fermentation was complete the acid was as clear and colorless as water. It would "make" if added to the cider vinegar, and next time will be used with it. The two acids combine well in flavor. I used the watermelon vinegar in making pickles and found it as successful as cider vinegar.

Fermentation may be started with yeast if one wants to make a vinegar without the flavor of the cider vinegar, and more quickly than by waiting for it to come as a natural result of conditions. Almost any liquid will turn to vinegar if left to sour and work itself clear. Molasses will become so acid that it must be diluted very much to use at all. I once made some pickles by pouring molasses over sliced green tomatoes—it was a recipe in a cook-book—and the resulting pickles were so sour that the acid made ordinary vinegar seem sweet. They could not be eaten, but might have been with diluted acid, perhaps.

Vinegars may be made from the juices of oranges, peaches, and other fruits. The recipes for these call for yeast-cake according to amount of liquid. Half a cake will ferment a gallon, or nature will do the same. There is no more real need for a fermentative agent than with watermelon. I have never made any of these fruit vinegars but have made many of the herb vinegars, and plan to keep mint and tarragon vinegar always on hand. With onions at the present price onion vinegar will be added to my supply of fancy vinegars. They may be made in quart quantities.

Eggs

There is an economy in putting down eggs for winter provided you can get absolutely fresh and infertile eggs. It will not pay to lay the eggs down unless you can be sure they are fresh. One of the leading authorities on farm matters has advised every one who can do so to put down eggs whenever they can be bought at less than forty cents a dozen, as the probability is that the price will rise in the future to much more than that. The price is lowest in spring when eggs are most abundant, but they are more liable then to be fertile and thus will not keep well.

There are several methods of preserving eggs, but the two tested by the

Department of Agriculture and recommended by the authorities of the Department are in water-glass and by lime. The country way for years was to put the eggs in a half-barrel or big lard-firkin. The great disadvantage of this is that the last eggs put down are the first to be eaten, unless one does as an old friend of mine did. When her firkin was full she put a tight lid on it and reversed it, opened it at the bottom and thus used the first laid down before the late. Better than that is to have smaller receptacles, which may be opened in order of age, beginning with the oldest. Working from the oldest to the last put down you will never get any that are very old.

Water-glass is a sodium silicate and is dissolved in water. The proper proportions are given with the material. The water has a somewhat slippery feeling. When the eggs are to be used, they are removed from the liquid and rinsed in clean, cold water, but must not wait long before being used. The information given by the Department of Agriculture says eggs thus preserved may be used for soft-boiling or poaching up to November. To cook an egg in the shell first prick a tiny hole in the large end of the shell with a needle to keep it from cracking. They are satisfactory for frying until December and after that time until March they may be used for omelets, custards, and cake cooking.

As the eggs become older, the whites become thinner and it is harder to separate yellow from white. It becomes difficult to beat the eggs. As the eggs age, they do not look as inviting and sometimes, even when not bad, there is a tinge of pink in the white, which is said to be due to a small supply of iron in the sodium silicate and does not harm the egg for cooking. Some of these changes in the eggs will be avoided by so placing them in separate receptacles that they do not get so old before using. Sixteen average-sized eggs may be packed with the water-glass in a half-gallon crock. Seal the jar or crock when full. The water-glass may be used again.

The most enthusiastic advocate of preserving eggs I ever met was a personal friend who had put eggs down in lime-water for forty years when she told me about that method. She did not like the water-glass method, and perhaps was slightly prejudiced against it, as she got better results with the lime-water. She said she had never had a bad egg with the lime process, but she was fortunate in having hens and thus being assured of perfectly fresh material to preserve. Forty years' experience and no poor eggs is a good recommendation. The lime-water is a strong solution, three pounds of unslaked lime to five gallons of water which has been boiled and allowed to stand until cool. The mixture must stand until the lime settles and the liquid is clear. The eggs are to be packed as with water-glass, having at least two inches of water above the eggs. Rinse as with the other preparation. These eggs retain their original appearance on breaking somewhat longer than the eggs from water-glass. The lime-water is somewhat the cheaper solution, but the Department of Agriculture endorses the water-glass process the more highly.

Eggs are so important a part of the family diet that it is well worth your time and care to have as many as you can. My grocer said, " The price of eggs in winter does not trouble me. In the spring I buy thirty dozen where I know they are good, put them down, and they last us until they come again." That is from a man who can always get his foods at cost price, and what is a good plan for him is equally good for others. Eggs must always be put down in earthenware or glass. I know I spoke of the firkin and have seen it used a great deal in the country, but it is like other exceptions to rules, and when you begin you do better to follow the rule exactly.

Buy no eggs for preserving which are over four days old. The fresher they are, the better for keeping.

Even when using fresh eggs, break each egg separately, and then only one will be lost. I once spoiled eight by breaking the ninth into them when it was much too old to be pleasant. Yolks separated from whites may be kept fresh if covered, without blending, with cold water. Cover the whites with a lid to keep from drying. If beaten eggs become hard, soften them with milk.

If eggs are scarce and you want to make a cake that calls for more than one egg, add the butter last and have it melted when added. Then one egg will serve for two cakes. Beat yolk and white separately and add last of all but the butter. Eggs may be made to do double duty by beating up with a tablespoonful of water to an egg. If more than three eggs are called for, omit one and add a spoonful of corn-starch. Beat it in with the eggs or the mixture may fall. It may be substituted in scrambled eggs or an omelet.

CHAPTER VI

THE GREATEST ECONOMY: YOURSELF

CHAPTER VI

THE GREATEST ECONOMY: YOURSELF

There is one possession which the woman who makes the greatest effort to be thrifty often wastes with reckless prodigality, in spite of the fact that it is so valuable it cannot be replaced by anything else; money cannot buy it, and once lost one seldom can get it again. Of all the wastes about the household this is the one irreparable, and as the housewife is wasting it she seems to think she is doing something very commendable. She will save her pennies and waste her life by overwork and lack of sleep, and in the end she spends all she has tried to accumulate, in the vain effort to be well again.

Of all the good gifts the fairies bestow

upon a child at birth, the first and best is good health; if that does not come by birth, the next best for the child is a mother wise enough to nurture him so heedfully that health grows within him as he sleeps, eats, and, later, works. Blessed is the household where the mother puts good health above all things except moral strength. In that household the mother does not throw away her strength and time doing work that can be eliminated, but she serves cleanliness with reason.

However hard one works and however steadily, she never can have an absolutely clean house. Nature forbids it. All out-of-doors is dirt, yet we take to out-of-doors and we thrive. Instead of working so hard to drive out the dust why not take more of out-of-doors into the house? That is thrift. It may fade the carpet, and the life-giving sunshine generally does fade it and the paper and other things, but these can be renewed if the members of the family are well, for they will work with so much more enthusiasm that their incomes will increase; moreover, there is no home that is so inviting and homelike as one that is not too new and speckless. Better is a home where faded walls and floor are, with a well, happy mother, than an immaculate, darkened home with an irritable, nervous mother presiding over it. In homes where the income is small, only one person to see to everything, there is always occasion to choose which you shall have, more show, more work, less happiness, or health and content with plain living. As a matter of dollars and cents, regardless of the spirit of the home—and the happiest homes are not the most scrubbed—it pays better to work less.

A woman will tell you, " I cleaned all my up-stairs to-day, took up the carpet, washed the floor, etc.," as if she had done a truly virtuous deed, when what she really did was to strain her back, neglect her food, work all day keyed at the highest tension, and go to bed at night with every nerve strained to the utmost, an aching head and back, and the consciousness that her weariness and aches have made her so snappy that the children have stayed as far from her as they could, and her husband has "decided to do some extra work at the office." Wearing one's self out like that and being cross is a sin, and if a woman herself must clean her house at such a cost she will be much wiser to let the extra work be undone. Probably no one else ever would know whether or not she had done all the cleaning, or care. Just why houses should become so remarkably dirty twice a year when they apparently have been kept clean all through the months between is one of the puzzles of a thoughtful mind.

When this country was first settled and only one fire was kept in most houses, and that in the kitchen, and all winter the family hibernated and dirt accumulated because it was too cold to clean the rooms unlived in, there was reason for a yearly digging-out; but now it is the custom to occupy all the house, and all is kept swept and garnished from January first, to the following December thirty-first at midnight it should be possible to keep it livable without any yearly upheaval. There is enough to be done each day not to add any needless labor to the amount.

If you, my dear sister-worker, find yourself getting so tired each day that you "cannot think," try this way of cultivating thrift. Take time to consider with yourself how not to waste your life. It is the best thing you have. Did you ever notice how many husbands have young wives spending the money saved by the work of the first wives, who die and leave it for their successors to spend? Why not spend it yourself? Reflect on that topic deeply and heartfully, and then decide first that you will not join the number of those thus making a place for some superfluous woman. That decision being made so that it cannot be shaken, reflect thoughtfully on what you can do to save yourself, which is to make yourself well and keep yourself well.

You know just about what you can do before you become conscious of weariness. You should stop a little the other side of that. If you can work but an hour and feel right, work that at your best and stop.

If you cannot afford to hire a helper—really cannot afford it by going without something else—then there remains for you only to cut down the work and have the members of your family help you. Probably you are the kind who hangs up everything the other members of the family drop, who puts away or packs everything for them, and who makes of herself an unthanked servant for the household. Having resolved to be just to yourself, you must change this condition, so talk over the situation with your family and request their coöperation in making life easier for you. Very likely they will be greatly surprised to know that you have any lacks in that respect. If you have brought them up so selfishly that they will not help for the asking, then make a demand that they do at least what belongs to them to do, the work they make, and if they do not heed your words, leave all their proper work undone.

Let their clothes lie where they were dropped, also their tennis-rackets, books, etc. Don't give way to the weakness of saying, "I can't stand seeing them around." If you can't, just go somewhere else and forget about them. You may as well go while you are able to do it as to wait until you are carried feet first. If you were sick abed you would have to let them lie, so play that you are too ill to attend to them. It should come easy to you to do that.

The woman who is always tired is a woman who is not well, and she belongs in bed quite as much as the woman who is there. Rest will do her more good than any medicine and help more to keep her well, and the housemother should rest some part of every day as soon as she is conscious of weariness; even fifteen minutes' relaxation will do her good, and after it she will go on with renewed energy. She can get this rest if she will. It is always possible to do the thing one should do, and to be pleasant is the first duty of a woman with husband and child.

As soon as you feel that you have more to do than you can ever get done, and wherever you turn you see nothing but dust and dirt, it is time for you to drop everything for half an hour. Go outdoors and breathe fresh air and see how the sky looks. There is no more dirt than when you did not notice it at all. You see it because your nerves are magnifying everything. Remember, "As thy days, so shall thy strength be," and you can do all that belongs to you to do without the wear that makes you cross. You have no more before you that absolutely must be done than you can do well. Separate the things you know *must* be done from those that can be left, and be guided in your decision by the state of your mind and body, and pay no heed to the things you would do because your neighbors do and think you should do. Your neighbors do not have your life to live; live it yourself as seems good to you. Tasks are the things you do to satisfy your neighbors'. notions. Do no more of them. They bring nervous prostration.

"Do the duty that lies nearest," but be sure it is a duty. You can recognize a duty because it is something that makes you and your family physically well, that develops them spiritually and morally, and does not take from you more than you are able to give. Your first duty is to make yourself so lovely that your family want to be with you. Nothing is worth while to you or them that does not help you to be dear to them. Test what you lay out for your work by its relation to this great demand, and reject it if it does not meet the test.

Very many seem-to-be-important tasks will fade into nothingness if judged by this test. You think of pies, doughnuts, cakes, or what else to be made, but are those really necessary to body or soul? They take much time and they are delicious, but if you are not strong, cannot

GREATEST ECONOMY: YOURSELF 101

your family be well nourished and wholesomely fed without them? You know they can. The actual requirements of the body to keep it in perfect physical trim are very few. A simple dietary does more to make and keep it perfect than all the products of the cook in sweets and desserts. All forms of thrift are against much cookery of that kind, thrift of time, money, strength, health, and good spirits.

Eggs, shortening, flour, milk, all are so expensive that it is not thrift to put much of them into the non-essentials of diet. While you deny your appetite these pleasing gratifications you can content yourself and family by reminding them of the gains in health, and in money. Very few women ever stop to reckon the cost of cakes or any such foods. They know what eggs and meat cost because they pay for them in a lump sum, but they cannot tell you what a cake costs until they count it up. With lard at twenty-five cents a pound, eggs at fifty cents or more a dozen, sugar nine cents or more a pound, and milk and flour equally high, it is not hard to see that cake is as expensive as needless. Women can lessen the indirect expenses of the family in many ways, beginning with what they need not spend on doctors and medicine.

If the housewife will cut out from her housework the non-essentials, she will go through her days much more healthfully and comfortably. Weariness creates poisons in the blood that after a while create the so-called diseases. Why not avoid the illness by leaving undone the acts that produce it? You will have to leave them undone after the illness; it is as easy to foresee the evil and escape it. One severe sickness will use up in a month the savings of a year and indirectly much more in what one's time is worth, and while the wages of the housewife's substitute are being paid as well as her board and breakages the appreciation of the regular worker's duties and value will be increasing.

"How shall I save health?" do you ask? "How shall I plan my days to eliminate the needless?" That is something no one can tell another, for the needs of families are different, but a general rule may be given. Simplify every department of life. With foods, cook those which are most easily prepared and use the fireless, since that is the easiest and least time-devouring of all cooking. That saves labor, time and money beside strength, all of which you need to conserve. Eat many uncooked articles for desserts; figs, raisins, dates, prunes, and other fruits cost less than cakes and puddings and keep the body in good tone. These are all good with the morning cereal. They supply also the sugar that is necessary for perfect nutrition.

Plan to have a meat or its substitute, a

starch, and a fat at each dinner. The body has to be fed with these to meet its needs. As most meals are provided for individuals of different ages and physical conditions, a compromise has to be arranged, varied as the mother knows to be best.

Meat substitutes are fish, fowl, cheese, nuts, legumes, milk and eggs. Potatoes and cereals furnish starches. Fats are found to some extent in most foods but the fats for the table are butter and cream, with salad oils, and children should be encouraged to eat much of them. Every family would be the healthier for a green salad daily which should be served without mayonnaise. There is no thrift in providing that dressing, which is as unwholesome as expensive. Many persons find peanut and cottonseed oil as pleasant as olive for salads and the cost is a third less. It is said that no case of appendicitis has ever developed among persons who eat oil freely. Children, unless they have heard their elders say they never could take oil, will eat vegetables dressed with oil and lemon juice and ask for more. There are so few fats palatable to children that the salad habit should be encouraged. Also, a salad is a dish easy to prepare for the table.

Economize on the daily duties by having those common to every day follow a regular routine. The more nearly automatic they become, the less they take out of you, while saving the wear of thinking, "What shall I do next?" Insist that each member of the family turn back his bed before leaving his room, and leave the window open. Also, have him take care of all his belongings. To pick up a paper or a match is not much effort, but it is as much for you as for him, and the aggregation of picking up for every one is an appreciable tax upon one. Perhaps the weaker sex would not be the weaker if she did not bend her back so much picking up what the stronger leaves on the floor. There will be more life for you to put into better things when you have taught your family to look after their own belongings. You should have begun the lessons when they were little. Each year of practice makes the good habit become more like instinct.

CHAPTER VII
LABOR-SAVING

CHAPTER VII
LABOR-SAVING

BEGIN on Sunday to prepare for the week's work so that you shall finish each day of it with the joy of doing, not with the weariness that grows greater and heavier day by day. Take your day of rest as does the man who insists on an eight-hour day. You need it as much as your men do. Plan your day's work and meals to be as light as you can possibly make them. Have your dinner nearly ready on Saturday. It won't hurt your men to eat cold meat once a week. Study how to get the hours of rest that will do you good; let it be your day and let your family make it good for you. Probably they will enjoy the change as much as you will, and you will feel and look so much the younger.

Take Monday to put the house in order after Sunday, to get food ready for wash-day; Tuesday, for putting clothes in soak and getting them ready thus to be treated. Monday is the day to take out the stains, to mend rents that will be enlarged by going through the wash, and to get the week well under way. It saves labor to soak the clothes with a good powder that you can make yourself, or to use a spoonful of kerosene to the gallon of water. The odor of kerosene will be lost when the clothes go through the wash. A washing-machine is an economy in the average household because it makes very hard labor become easy and does the same work in half the time. Add a good wringer, and wash-day is no more to be dreaded than any other day. Laundry work is the hardest and most exacting of the household, and a woman should have every appliance that will make it easier, if to have them she leaves her bedroom with only a bed, table, and chair.

When you put the clothes on the line hang all things of the same kind together, all sheets, slips, etc., side by side. Hang them to swing smoothly, and fold as taken from the line. Do not iron. Sun-dried sheets folded while the sun is on them are so sweet that ironing is no improvement. Moreover, there is health in such clothing. Fold ordinary towels and do not iron them. For underwear, woven garments, or those made of crêpe or seersucker if you want heavier material, will need no ironing, just pulling into smoothness and shape. They are very pretty with a little needlework for trimming, which may be done in odd minutes. By a little thought you can make your ironing only a small amount of work, less than the washing.

If you do your own work, all that you can leave undone without lessening the comfort or in any degree injuring the health of your family will keep you fresher and happier. If you hire your laundry done, the less ironing, the less the cost for the washing, and the more you will have for the finer things of the mind or for charity. To-day from all over the world comes the cry for help, and to answer it one must practise thrift as never before.

Try to have as few handlings of the clothes as you can. You can sort the not-to-be-ironed as you take from the line. As you iron the others, place systematically on the drier. Have those to be mended separated from the others on the drier and so on. Mend when taken from the drier, and do not put anything away without buttons on and rents repaired. Let the sewing-machine help with the mending. Do not waste time sewing by hand when it can be more effectively done by machine.

If you have a small family, you may save time and strength by doing your dishes all at one time. Scrape them, pile in an orderly manner, pour hot water over them, and let them stand in the pan until the most convenient hour of your day for doing them. This may be in the pauses of getting dinner at night. There is a considerable saving of time, and the dishes by their soaking are about half-washed when one begins on them.

It will be a great help in keeping rooms clean to have on each floor a duster, broom, and brush. By removing dust and dirt as it comes the weekly cleaning may be turned into a fortnightly work, and made easier by taking half of the rooms each week. With your work, as with your money, it is the small savings and expenditures that count for profit or loss. Use your head to devise methods of saving motions and labor. Keeping things convenient is a great gain in health.

In your kitchen and pantry have your cooking articles and dishes so arranged that you can get what you want without moving anything else, and all within easy reach. That is a decided advantage in working rapidly, and is free from the irritating influence that accompanies keeping dishes, covers, and so on, piled one on another.

CHAPTER VIII
BREAD AND CAKE

CHAPTER VIII

BREAD AND CAKE

BREAD, being the commonest and most important article of food, must form a large part of the cost of the table. In no other thing has the standard of the housewife changed so greatly as in relation to bread-making. One of the memories from my childhood in New England is hearing the discussion of a woman new to the neighborhood, and what I remember is this, spoken in pitying accents: "Yes, poor thing, she does the best she can, but she hasn't any faculty. Why, *she buys her bread!*" That to the generation earlier was a sure indication of a poor or lazy housewife. Now it is the exceptional housekeeper who makes her own bread, and perhaps that fact has had its share in raising the cost of living.

Whether it were more profitable to make my bread, cake, and other flour products or to buy them, no one was able to tell me when I began to keep house, so I determined to find out for myself, and I kept account of all that was baked from a bag of flour, added to that the cost of other material and of fuel. As gas has always been my fuel and I can read my meter I could tell how much gas was burned for each baking or steaming. I found a gain of fifty per cent., and if there were no gain where would the baker get his profit? Though he buys for less and has increased production, he must pay other expenses lacking to the housewife, so it is fair to credit him with a cost no heavier than that of the home-maker, and his profit she saves when she does the work. No housewife at the head of a large family can afford to buy her bread if she desires to be thrifty in the least. The higher the price of flour and other material, the more need of her being the bread-maker.

The following statement may help you to see that making your bread is cheaper than buying it, outside of the fact that home-made bread has more body to it than baker's bread, and " goes farther." In a barrel of flour there will be flour enough for 330 loaves of bread. Suppose you pay $15 for the flour. Your loaves at ten cents each, and they are quite as likely to be more, will cost $33, and you will see at once that the shortening and baking will not cost you any such sum as the difference between cost of the barrel of flour and cost of loaves of bread bought from the baker. A light, delicious loaf of home-made bread will serve more than baker's bread because it has more substance to it. No woman with a family of four persons is thrifty if she buys bread unless she is frail and overburdened with work.

In my family of three persons I have found it profitable to make my cakes, pies, breads, and puddings, planning to bake when there is something else to cook at the same time. With gas for fuel, it is wasteful to run the oven for only one article. It takes as much gas to bake a roast as to bake a roast, a loaf, potatoes, and one other thing, which are all a gas oven will hold.

Good bread, even the much-vilified fine white bread, has considerable food value. An expert on nutrition (Brewster) says a slice of it toasted and buttered has as much nutriment as an egg.

"As for the vexed question of Graham and entire-wheat bread vs. white, the difference is really not nearly so great as some persons would have us believe. In fuel value, the white has a slight advantage, since the darker forms are commonly made up with somewhat more water. The protein of the darker sorts amounts, on the average, to only about two per cent. more, fifty bites of the one matching forty-nine of the other. The white sorts are for most persons distinctly more digestible. In the bone-building minerals the difference is somewhat greater. Even here it amounts, in general, to only about two parts in ten. Moreover, some white flour contains more protein and more phosphates than some dark, the low-grade flours having commonly the most. The striking difference between white and dark flours lies in their content of woody fibre, which may be twenty times as great in certain brands of Graham as is the super-refined white. This fibre tends to make the bread indigestible. On the other hand, there is probably nothing else so good for keeping the bowels properly at work."

Thus does Brewster dispose of a favorite popular notion. Recent investigations among English workingmen show that among well-nourished men of that class, bread provides nearly two-thirds of the total energy value of the ration. This proves that bread is worthy of its high place in the dietary, and the more active the individual, the better for him is bread. "The mainstay of a child's diet should be bread." He is always working, and the bread and butter give him what he needs in the best form. There is good basis for the Continental breakfast of bread and coffee or chocolate, and workers of the offices and stores who have tried for breakfast two slices of buttered toast, with fruit cooked or raw, will rarely return to the heavier meal, which makes the mind heavier as well.

Do not have always the same kind of bread. Variety in this is as welcome as in other things and as readily found. You may have bran, rice, whole wheat, brown bread, as part of your bread ration and it will pay you to make it yourself. Then for breads that are almost a meal in themselves offer nut, date, and raisin bread. These need no meat accompaniment and will satisfy hunger perfectly. Where lunches have to be put up daily, these breads should be made often. Nut bread with butter or jam is the delight of all who have been given it.

Bread become stale is bread in its most wholesome state. It is amazing how slight a realization most women have of the uses of stale bread. Not a crumb should be thrown away. In this one article the housewife will find herself gaining greatly in thrift as she learns how to avail herself of crumbs and broken bread. Even the crumbs that remain on the bread-board after cutting should be turned into a glass jar. Dried slowly without browning, they will keep indefinitely and are ready for any number of purposes, saving cracker crumbs. All crumbs, all bits of bread, and heels of loaves should be dried thoroughly, ground fine with a bread-roller or through a meat-grinder, and they are even better than the cracker crumbs one buys for breading cutlets, etc. The lightest griddle-cakes have bread crumbs as their foundation; brown bread is all the better for having part of the wheat flour added as crumbs.

The delicious bread sauce so favored in England with roast chicken cannot be made without bread crumbs; they may be combined with potatoes for frying if there is a scant supply of the latter; a hash is improved if crumbs take the place of part potato; bread crumbs are needed in all households for breading cutlets, croquettes, chops and such things. Bread crumbs help well to fill out a meal when combined with mashed potato, blended with an egg, all seasoned,

BREAD AND CAKE

shaped in small balls and dropped in deep hot fat.

A dish of considerable substance may be prepared from crumbs by soaking them in a cup of milk, adding an egg, seasoning well, then adding a spoonful of baking-powder and enough flour to make a thin batter. Into this stir any bits of meat you have—if it is only a spoonful it will give flavor.

Shavings of fat pork, nice and brown, are very good. You can turn the batter over the fat pork-crisps and bake them like pancakes. If you cook on top of the stove, when one side is brown, turn it and brown the other. It can be baked in the oven also. You can have a hearty, appetizing dish by having some bacon in the skillet with the fat and turning the batter over it. Have plenty of fat but not too much, which is when it comes above the dough. To have crumbs prepared is a saving of time and a great convenience. Crumbs for scallops should be bigger than for breading. Always make the dough for anything of which crumbs are a part somewhat thicker than with flour alone. Crumbs may be mixed with a custard and "make it go farther" without making it less palatable.

Probably there is more unthrift connected with the treatment of stale bread than in any one other branch of family service. Garbage men can tell how seldom does one find a garbage pail that does not hold enough of bread alone to feed a hungry man for a day, and that is a low limit, as any one knows who has shared the garbage receptacle of an apartment house. Stale bread toasted, dressed with a white sauce to which grated cheese has been added, makes a dish with nutrition enough for the breakfast of a man who works out-of-doors. In Europe, cheese and bread are an important part of the diet and may well help those who wish

BREAD AND CAKE

to make thrift take the place of dollars. Slices of cheese are served for breakfast in some parts of Europe just as slices of cold meat sometimes are served in the United States.

Crumbs of brown bread and corn-meal bread may be converted into baked Indian pudding by substituting them for part of the meal the recipe calls for. Then follow the rule. If you have any dry gingerbread add that to the other. Bread puddings are very good when well made; when not they are a waste of material. There are many kinds of excellent puddings which will use the crumbs, but a bread pudding which calls for several eggs should be made very seldom. Puddings are served after the appetite is satisfied or nearly so, and the nutrition of the meal does not require eggs; when the main part of the meal has been light, a two-egg pudding is more thrifty than at other times because there is need of more food value in the dessert. Eggs are not extravagant when they are a substitute for meat, but except when of low cost, are wasteful in puddings and cakes because they are added to a meal which does not need them.

Cake cannot be called a necessity of life but it is a food that is pleasant and has considerable nutrition, therefore it may have an occasional place on the table of the thrifty, though as it is always eaten after a fulness of other food, it should be a simple combination of one egg, or two at most, with such ingredients as one needs. As good a cake as any family need to eat may be made with two eggs; if you make simple cakes for daily fare you will not mind the expense of something richer on festal occasions.

Most experienced housewives have a recipe which has proved worth making up, and this they vary as they need other cakes. For instance, gingerbread by the following rule has been made in our family for years and is thoroughly dependable. You will note that it is eggless. One-half cup of molasses, one-fourth cup sugar, one-fourth cup melted shortening; turn on these one-half cup of boiling—not just hot—water. I use coffee left from breakfast in place of the water if there is any. Allow enough flour to make a slightly thick batter (about two cups, more or less), with which sift one-half teaspoonful each of soda, salt, and ginger. Bake slowly, as any molasses mixture burns readily. This is turned into a bake-sheet and baked about two inches thick. That is the first result.

From this come other cakes. Sometimes I bake in muffin tins and have little cakes; sometimes to the original recipe I add raisins, or chopped dates, or citron, or any two of these; sometimes I **turn a cup of black walnut meats broken**

rather fine into the dough, and
delicious. Then I season with s]
fruit cake, and add nuts, raisins
little minced orange peel that I c
I made my Christmas plum pud
a variation of this recipe and i1
good as any Christmas puddin{
to be.

Beside being plain gingerbread
cakes it is made in layers; as a la)
it does not need as much flour.
supper dessert, I have it hot anc
between the layers jelly or v
cream when I have something l(
my week's allowance. Sometimes
a nut or other filling. Sometimes
it as a loaf. As my oven is li
burn on the bottom, I bake my
my iron skillet and it makes a
loaf of extra size. You see what
by an inexpensive base producin
cakes. You can turn this into
chocolate cake by omitting the

and using an ounce of cake chocolate, or two spoonfuls of powdered cocoa or chocolate with it, and seasoning with vanilla. By frosting with chocolate or other icing you will have a cake that seems much more expensive than it is. It is the same cake in all forms but it does not taste the same and in all it is inexpensive. Of course, as nuts and fruits go into it the cost rises. Gingerbread is the most desirable form of cake for home consumption—speaking from the health point—and served hot will delight nearly every one. There are recipes for its making requiring from no eggs to four, and for keeping it is well to add an egg, but gingerbread never keeps with us. It is so good that it quickly disappears.

It is very well to use several eggs in a cake or pudding if one serves it when there is very little preceding it as food, but not otherwise. When one has satisfied his appetite with heavier food the system does not need the protein of the eggs and it is mainly wasted. There are many good eggless recipes, much to the purpose with eggs at fifty to sixty cents a dozen, or even more. Eggs as the main dish of a meal are not extravagant, even at the higher price, but as part of cakes and puddings they are not used in our house when they go above forty-five cents a dozen, and very seldom at that price. The members of my family do not know whether my cake is made with eggs or not, but they say " it tastes like more."

CHAPTER IX
SOUPS

CHAPTER IX

SOUPS

HOUSEWIVES in this country do not know as they should the thrift of soups. They understand the merits of chowders and stews which are dishes containing everything for a meal in one composition, but they have never really grasped the economy of a thin soup daily at the beginning of a dinner. It is truly economical. It warms the stomach and starts the digestive apparatus as surely as does drinking warm water before eating. Its work is very much the same. If one is very hungry, it takes the edge off the appetite, and that is more healthful than eating as we do when we are very hungry.

Less meat is eaten when soup is served, and the body thrives as well. As a rule, the ordinary household does not serve soups as a first course of a dinner, seeming to regard it as a luxury for the table of the rich, whereas it is one of the greatest economies. It is rarely necessary to buy material for the daily soup. In my household nothing except an occasional bunch of soup herbs was bought for soup in a year. The bones from different meats and fowl supplied the stock, and left-overs of vegetables gave variety.

Cream soups are too heavy for a first course unless the second be of vegetables or the less nourishing fish. With salmon or oily fish it is a bad arrangement. As an economy, one should not make cream soups often. Water in which vegetables are boiled should be the base of soups. French housewives do not add meat juices to this. The water with a little of the vegetable in it is seasoned and served with sippets of bread as the first course. To American palates it seems flat at first, but not after a while, and the water contains mineral salts which are beneficial to the taker of them. You can make your soup look better to you by thickening it with corn-starch or flour to what you like as soup consistency, and you can add milk if you like it better that way. Season it well, serve with it croutons, which are dice of stale bread browned in butter or bacon fat. Then you will have a good soup.

Did you know you could make nice soup from left-overs of fish? One of the nicest I ever had or ate was the result of an experiment of mine. I boiled the backbone and skin of a cooked finnan-haddie for half or three-quarters of an hour in water; strained it, seasoned with butter and salt, added milk to make soup enough for serving, and passed toasted crackers with it. That was made from what seemed to be wholly waste, and the family declared it as good as oyster

138 THRIFT IN THE HOUSEH

soup. Milk may be added to a
except meat stock, and it makes
richer in food value.

Unless one has the art of maki
from the little leavings that cann
wise serve the family there is 1
omy in having them, but it will
housekeeper to acquire the k1
making good soup from the bits
soups, well seasoned, are very g
should be more frequently served
require milk for the body of t
and are heartier than vegetable-s
which water is the stock.

The cook who wishes to sur
fellows must become past mis
the art of seasoning. She will
ferent spices for different soups
have everything taste alike. Cor
cooks, even to the humblest mot
home, know how to season, and
sult is a flavor compounded of r
gredients, not one of which is

than another. One will use a single clove or peppercorn, a leaf of celery, and so on, the whole being so delicious to the smell that one is made eager to eat it.

Soups are always thin, about as thin as milk; the next member of the soup family is a purée, which is a thick soup, but not thick enough nor compounded to be a stew; then come chowders and stews, which are really meals of themselves, not, like purées and soups, aids to a meal. Purées of the legumes, that is, peas, beans of all varieties, and lentils, are heavy enough, though made only of one ingredient beside water and seasoning, to form a meal with bread and butter that is as hearty as an ordinary woman should eat at luncheon. These need long cooking, and should be started with soaking overnight. The more they are cooked, the more wholesome they are, though they need not measure up to the time set by Mother Goose for her bean porridge.

The national dish of France and also of Belgium is a kind of chowder, though called soup, because it never would be a course at a dinner. As you would expect, the *pot au-feu*, and *huitze pot* are masterpieces of thrift, and as the need in this country for cheap living increases there can be no better aid to meeting that need than to learn to make either of these soups. They are alike in their general making, for which there is no rule. No one buys new material for these soups; they are a combination of what cannot go on the table, because there may not be enough of it. The stock pot in a French or Belgian family is never empty, unless for an occasional washing. Into it go the left-overs, a bean-pod, a leaf of cabbage or lettuce, the bones from the meat—these are rather few —a sausage, and so on. In our country the garbage pail gets all of these, for it is the little bit that makes the *pot au-feu* and the *huitze pot*, and all the bits feed those who without them would go hungry. Then the pot receives the water it needs, and everything simmers away for hours, so slowly that nothing is spoiled by hard boiling; another agency for the appetizing result is the flavoring. That cannot be imparted by directions, but any one can learn it by experimenting.

Before the War, one would see in the markets the children of the very poor gleaning from the floor of the marketplace the scraps that would furnish the *huitze pot* and save them from hunger. It would not seem that these bits of refuse could be made of any service, but a bean-pod is not the less something to eat because it has fallen to the ground, and so the poor are fed, for the children would collect a basketful of odds and ends that no one begrudged them, and no one else wanted. It is a thrifty people that teaches its poor to make something worth eating from what it finds to its hand. Our people should learn the same lesson of thrift, though perhaps not the same application of it.

Chowders and thick soups should be eaten as the hearty dish of a meal, and should not be preceded by a soup. They supply all the nutrition and bulk that the system needs at a meal. After the legumes have been strained, do not throw away the pulp which has a great deal of the peas, beans, or lentils still with it. Shape it into a mold around a platter and fill the space with sauerkraut or with left-over meat minced and thickened with white or brown sauce, or tomato made solid with gelatine, or chopped cabbage and beets, or sliced onions and cucumbers, or cabbage with diced celery and apples, or whatever occurs to you. If you have seasoned everything well, so that it tastes right without being spiced much, your family will not miss meat when this is served. First you will have your soup, then the dish which is so pretty with the mold and contrasting center, and if you add to this some corn-meal muffins or johnny-cake, so much the better, with a light dessert for finish. This is a very satisfactory dinner for active workers, but a little heavy for sedentary workers if taken in the middle of the day.

Either chowders or stews may be baked if preferred. When they are baked in a casserole or bean-pot there is less of the waste that goes into the air. The economy of any food requiring much cooking depends somewhat upon the nature of the fuel. If you keep a coal fire for its heating value, any cooking you may do on it is so much gained, while if gas or electricity is your fuel, cooking is an extra cost and the amount may be estimated by watching the meter. It might be much cheaper to provide a food of which the first cost was considerably more than that of peas or beans, but the cooking expense very much less. When you have made your fireless cooker you will find stews, chowders, and such foods very nutritious and as inexpensive, as the cost of cooking by fireless is so trifling. If you want to keep a greater heat in the cooker, place at the bottom under your kettle a brick or two heated as hot as is safe. If you have an old blanket or carpet you can throw over the entire outside, so much the better.

All gravies are a good starting-point for a soup. Let it make the soup for your first course. Dilute it to proper consistency, season with whatever you have, add any left-over vegetable of which there is only a spoonful or two, or even a spoonful of the cereal from breakfast which will thicken it somewhat. Simmer it for a couple of hours, strain, add croutons, or noodles, and serve.

Make only enough for one meal at a time. When there is gravy, it may be added to the water in which a yesterday's vegetable was boiled. If there is no gravy, milk may be the base of the soup flavored with the water for the vegetables.

If you think a soup so compounded will not be worth serving, try this which I served yesterday. The spinach for dinner was cooked only in the water that clung to its leaves, but as it cooks, the steam brings out more, and when the spinach is done there will be a pint of liquid. This contains the mineral salts which are so valuable for the body. Spinach furnishes iron, and unless one gets some part of the liquid, all of this is lost. To my mind, it is better economy to administer iron in this way than as a drug. This liquor was hot, salted, half a pint of milk added, the bits of the vegetable left in the soup, and a nicer light soup you will not often find. One of the best arguments for saving the water in which vegetables are cooked is the eating of the wholesome part of the vegetable, otherwise lost.

A simple soup may be made from the liquor that surrounds canned peas. Add to it two tablespoonfuls of peas mashed through a sieve. Put the liquid and the mashed peas into a pan with a scant pint of milk and a thickening of corn-starch. Cook only long enough to remove the rawness of the corn-starch. Season, and serve with croutons. This soup is rich in nutrition.

If you want to increase the nutriment of a soup, serve it with grated cheese, for which you can use the hard cheese not fit for serving at table as cheese with dessert. You can even make a cheese soup if you wish which will be too nourishing to be served with much else for a meal. The foundation is milk and water, in equal parts, brought to the boiling-point, thickened with flour or corn-starch in the proportion of a tablespoonful to a quart. When this is cooked and seasoned with paprika, mustard, and salt to suit taste, add two tablespoonfuls of grated cheese to a quart. Serve with cubes of hot toast, or toasted crackers, and you have a good supper for a cold night.

CHAPTER X

OILS AND FATS

CHAPTER X

OILS AND FATS

OILS and fats are important articles in the family diet and at the present time are mounting in price so rapidly that to supply them becomes a real problem. To the woman who regards lard as the only material to be considered for shortening and frying, there is nothing to be said, but there are other fats equally good or better, and the systematic saving and clarifying of fats brought out in cooking will lessen very considerably the amount that must be bought.

Save water in which meat has been boiled, and let it cool with the fat in it. It will rise to the top, become a firm cake which may be removed, freed from any scum at the under side, and will be as good for most cooking as the fat you pay well for. Before cooking sausage scald it with boiling water. Let it stand. Grease will cover the top of the water. Remove the sausage, turn the water into an open jar with large top, and treat the fat that forms into cake in the same manner as the other. This will be flavored with spices, but it is very excellent shortening for dark cakes and gingerbread. It is good for frying potatoes, but cannot be as generally used for shortening as the fat from beef and pork.

All fat from cooking should be saved and clarified; to clear it, put over the fire and heat until the water evaporates, being careful that the fat neither discolors nor burns. An easier method is to boil all fats in water, salt when taking from the heat, and let it cool on the water. Fat so cleared is always white. If bits of skin, etc., are caught in it when cooling, strain through a clean cloth or very fine sieve.

You can strain water and all, and the fat will separate so that it needs no further care except to take it from the water. This fat may be used acceptably in place of butter and lard.

Fat from lamb and mutton will lose its objectionable features if mixed in the proportion of one-third lamb or mutton fat and two-thirds beef or pork fat. Chicken fat is one of the very best of fats, and when mixed with beef and pork fat it looks like butter. It does not injure fats for cooking to be combined. Chicken fat should be tried out like others, and if a fowl is very fat the excess should not be cooked with the bird but reserved for cooking. It may be used for cakes, puddings, and biscuits, and gives no hint of any unpleasant flavor. As the fat of suet is rather hard when cool, that of poultry is well mixed with it to lighten it.

Suet is a wholesome fat and should form part of the family's material much oftener than it does. To use it is true thrift. When it is chopped very fine it makes good shortening for puddings and the crust of meat pies. It is not good shortening for things to be eaten cold because it coagulates as it cools. Suet tried out is white and inviting. It can be used exactly as lard is and for the same purposes. It may take the place of butter in sauces and gravies. Its value in the household economy should be better known. Its first cost is the lowest of all cooking fats except mutton, which owing to its tendency to form a coating on whatever it touches, can be used only in combination with other fats.

One housekeeper, with some local renown as a cook, uses suet entirely in her cooking. She buys at the rate of two pounds for fifteen cents, tries it out with water, and has something over a pound and a half of very nice shortening. The fat tried out from the suet known as

OILS AND FATS

cord-fat is no stiffer than good lard. Cord-fat is the fat about the intestines and costs less than some other, and harder suet. Suet works very well mixed with lard or vegetable oil in any proportion.

Bacon fat has so much merit that not a drop of it should be wasted. The French use it in salad dressing, and like it better than any other oil for that purpose. It may serve very well in many ways not commonly known. It may be the shortening for gingerbread, or it may even be used to enrich biscuit, and you will be surprised to find that there will be no bacon taste to the biscuit unless you have let the fat become browned. It rather improves corn-bread to have the seasoning of bacon, and it seems to be a richer shortening than lard in the same quantity. I have seen a housekeeper who always talks about the high cost of living and who earnestly strives to lessen her part of it empty into her sink all the grease from the breakfast bacon. She did not know she could use it for anything but frying potatoes, and she did not know that she could keep it sweet as long as lard if she kept it cool and clean. When you empty the skillet in which you have been frying bacon, do not wash it. Have some griddle-cakes for breakfast, or something else to use up the fat that does not run from the skillet. You will have more left in it than you realize, so why throw away a fat and then be obliged to replace by some more that which you wasted? Do not leave the skillet standing day after day with left-over grease in it, as that will attract bugs and hold dirt, but plan to use it the next meal, for an omelet or any one of the many things you cook in a greased skillet.

Vegetable oils steadily make their way in popular favor, and though the first cost seems rather more it really is not, for only half as much of the oils for cooking are used in any recipe as the amount of butter or lard given in the recipe as necessary. Dietists claim a wholesomeness for the vegetable oils that is lacking to the animal oils. They give a very pleasant flavor and a delightful brownness to whatever is fried in them.

In frying, it really is cheaper to use a deep fat—this is the true frying—enough to cover the article to be cooked by it, than to use only surface fat, renewing as it disappears. At best it is a wasteful manner of cooking with the arguments many and strong against it for health's sake. Anything that soaks fat and leaves grease on the plate is unfit for food. For the thrifty, frying will never be a favorite method of cooking, but for croquettes and some other articles one must use it now and then. When frying, do not let the fat get smoking hot and stand waiting for the cook to use it. Be ready before the fat is, and drop into it only a little at a time, since its temperature falls with each cold spoonful put into it. This is not only an economy of fat, but is the only way of keeping an even temperature for the articles plunged into it.

One fat preparation against which prejudice has done much deserves better treatment than it has had, and if once tested in a family remains there. Thousands of families who have to buy poor butter, really unfit for eating, refuse to try oleomargarine because they have read so much against it written by those interested in selling butter, and with them it is like,

> " No man e'er felt the halter draw,
> With good opinion of the law."

The butter interest is rich, and it has printed much against oleomargarine that is not just, and it has succeeded in making a heavy penalty fall on the merchant who sells it colored like butter. There is now a heavy tax on each pound of colored oleomargarine. I have a friend who ate oleomargarine for two years, paying thirty-five cents a pound as she supposed for butter. That is the argument of the butter-sellers against it. It cuts out the sale of butter, but to the man whose salary is twenty dollars a week or less, that does not seem an argument against it when a good sweet butter costs him from forty-five cents a pound upwards, and then does not keep as sweet as oleo does.

Oleo is a more cleanly fat than cheap, worked-over butters, and has been improved so greatly that if Congress had not hurt its sale by establishing for it a standard of whiteness strongly prejudicial to it in the customer's eyes, thousands now would be eating it to their decided advantage who now go without eating any butter fat or else buy what they cannot afford to buy. One would object to eating the uncolored oleo just as he objects to eating white butter. There is no law against coloring that. Makers are allowed to color butter without stating on the wrapper that it has been so treated. Why this is permitted and such restriction placed on coloring oleomargarine with the same ingredient is one of the peculiarities of legislation which affect the buyer uncomfortably and make him somewhat cynical when he reads of "equal rights for all." To him it seems to indicate that really there is quite a difference between tweedledum and tweedledee.

June butter gives naturally the color that the eye craves, but only June butter has it, from the quality of new grass. It would be impossible to make enough butter in one month to supply the demand during the year, and some milk would not give it at all, but as the public will not buy white butter, all butter-makers are allowed to color it at their desire in order to increase the selling properties of their product, which is the same reason that the makers of oleomargarine want to use it, and would if it were not for the weight of the influence of the butter-makers. The coloring is vegetable and may be used with perfect safety. In fact, a bottle of coloring may be sold with the uncolored oleomargarine which the buyer may mix with it, and that is lawful. Isn't that interesting, consistent, and amusing?

If one does not want oleomargarine he will not buy it even if it is colored, but next to butter, it is the best preparation, and it is so good a butter substitute that you cannot tell the difference sometimes, therefore I advise the use of it for those who seek thrift. Recently I had some butter at fifty-four cents a pound and some oleomargarine at twenty-seven, and those at the table could not tell by taste or eye which was the butter. In cooking anything, there is a separation in the hot fat that proves it to be oleomargarine, but does not affect the flavor at all.

In England, the meat drippings are sold in small groceries and the poor buy that instead of butter. Others beside the poor buy it. "Spread bread with drippings and toast it in the oven and you will find it a very good dish," said an Englishwoman to me. Equally good will you find it to take your stale bread, spread over it the crisp scraps that are left after frying out the fat of suet, and toasting these and bread together in a good oven. There is no need for butter substitute beyond these. Try it some cold night for supper with some vegetable accompaniment. It will be very nice with the bean soup or other legumes.

These crisp scraps are also very pleasant to the taste stirred into corn-meal breads before baking. No other shortening will be necessary.

There is something else to be considered from fats, and that is the economy of turning the waste fats into soap. Fats that are not clean enough for eating may be converted into soap with as little labor as to make bread. You can, if you wish, make several dollars' worth of good soap for no greater expense than the potash used with the fat. If you think you will try it, have a receptacle for scraps of cooked fats, trimming of meats that cannot be tried out for table use, what is left after trying out all suet, extra amounts of mutton fat, which is very agreeable to the skin, and when you have six pounds you will be ready to make your soap.

Have at hand a tin of reliable potash. Dissolve the lye in three quarts of cold water in a large kettle on the back of the stove, then put in the scraps and boil until they seem to be dissolved. You will be surprised to see how they will be converted by the lye. Strain the liquid through a sieve. Boil the scraps about ten minutes with a little water to draw from them what they retain, and add to the first water. Throw the scraps away. Put the other part on the stove to boil until it is converted into soap and looks like a very thick cream. When it reaches this stage add one-third cup pure borax dissolved in a little water, and one-half cup of ammonia. Be very careful it does not boil over, which it does quickly, and stir with a wooden spoon. When you take it from the stove, stir into it one-half cup of sugar to make it like froth, stir well for five minutes, then turn into dish to cool. You can put it into a wide-mouthed stone crock and cut a slice as you want it. This soap is not as hard as bar soap and harder than soft soap. It is for kitchen use wholly. If any liquid settles, you can use it for floors or for putting clothes to soak.

On all tins of good lye there will be

found a recipe for making soap, not all having the same recipe, but the one I have given is one which has been used for years in one family, and has been found serviceable without being hard on the hands. Excess of lye will make any soap bad for the skin, but the proportion given is not severe.

If you do not care to serve thrift by making your year's supply of soap for about fifty cents, take the waste scraps you would have used in this way and keep them wrapped in paper in a thick paper bag; when you want a quick fire or to kindle your fire use these scraps. Of course you must not keep many on hand as they will corrupt, but for rapid heat they are excellent.

CHAPTER XI
COAL AND ICE

CHAPTER XI

COAL AND ICE

The cost of fuel is a very heavy expense in all families, and the less one knows about how to run a fire, the heavier the expense. Knowledge is economy in warming a house and getting the heat for which one has paid. The greatest economy in fuel is that which is given by proper running of the fire. Few know how; those who do know can heat their houses on a much smaller amount of coal. Those who do not want heavy coal bills will show thrift by living in a sunny house and letting every bit of sunshine get into the rooms. That makes a perceptible difference in the amount of coal one burns.

The fire-pot of the stove or furnace should never be heaped to the top, but the coal always kept on the line of the fire-brick. All coal above that is wasted, and by obstructing the draft lessens the heat obtained. Those who do not know how to get heat out of coal always pile the stove full and learn nothing by experience. The coal should be started so that the gas shall be burned off gradually, then the furnace or range regulated so that the coal burns steadily without burning fast. It is the rapid, almost white-hot fire burning out at once that forms clinkers, which are always the indication of uneven firing.

In warming a house it is not necessary to be throwing coal on almost as often as one would throw wood, and when a furnace is fired in that way it is a waste of fuel, heat, and money. It is an economy to sift ashes if one burns coal in such a fashion that a large part of it is left unburned, but it is a much greater economy to burn it in such a manner that no cinders and no unburned or half-burned coal remain to be burned again. The art of running a coal fire has to be learned by practice, and you have it when you do not find stove or furnace filled with cinders or half-burned coal.

When we began our housekeeping neither of us knew anything about a furnace or what coal to buy, and what we did get vanished with a saddening rapidity. More than that, the furnace fire went out regularly each day, but "knowledge is power" with furnaces as with other things and both members of the family proceeded to get knowledge experimentally and by asking others. Now we know how to run a furnace and keep warm on as small amount of coal as any one we know. If we found those who could do it for less we should at once learn from them. Why burn ten tons of coal if nine can be made to furnish the necessary heat?

We started our career as firemen with kitchen and furnace coal, big pieces which filled the fire-box and burned with discouraging quickness. One of our consulted said, "Why don't you try pea coal?" That is a very small coal, and when we tried it it fell through the grate almost as fast as it went in at the top. Further consultation led to starting the fire with a good bed of furnace coal over which the small coal is laid. The small coal forms a bed on which more is laid, and once we learned how, it was thoroughly satisfactory for heat, for lasting, and for cost, as pea coal is much less dear than the larger coal, and though you get no more pounds for the money, what you do get seems to go farther. The fire has kept eighteen hours without attention and then burned up.

In our endeavors to find warmth at a reasonable rate we tried coke which had been recommended to us, but we did not like it as well as the pea coal. Coke as recommended to us would be mixed, one part of coke to two parts of coal. It worked fairly well, making a hot fire which was soon exhausted. Burned in any larger proportion, it soon burns out the fire-box because it gives such an intense heat. There is the further disadvantage of having to renew fuel much more frequently than with coal alone, and this extra amount burned serves to offset considerably any apparent saving in first cost. Our experience in burning coke was that coke was an expensive and unsatisfactory fuel, increasing labor and dirt.

Any woman who wants merely to keep a fire going in her kitchen should be able to hold the fire on a large hodful of coal a day. The average kitchen maid will burn four hodfuls to produce the same effect. When not intending to use the fire for cooking, just keep it alive and increase the heat gradually as needed, and your part in the cost of coal will lessen with no decrease in the efficiency of what is burned. It is less expensive to keep a furnace fire going than to build it, but if one is going to cook much when a great heat is desired in the oven it is better to start a new fire in the range. Much less coal will keep a fire than will start it, therefore let your effort for thrift influence you to get well acquainted with the idiosyncrasies of your furnace and range. If you are at all imaginative, long before you have mastered it you will believe firmly in "the total depravity of inanimate things," and that your furnace is the worst, but as you learn what it can do you will forget all that and be ready to tell your neighbors how you can produce wonderful results instead of discomfort.

If you have poor coal you may find it better to sift your ashes. Some coal is more wasteful than others. It is cheaper also to buy of some dealers than of others whose prices are less. Slate is cheaper than coal in cash but not for long. Get a good dealer and stick to him. Buy your coal if you possibly can during the summer months when prices are lowest, and buy your year's supply then. Sometimes you can buy it without having it all delivered at once, but sent to you as you need it, in two-ton loads. If you own your house and live where cold winters are, you will find it a decided economy to put double windows on the cold side of the house. A Maine man once told me that in one winter he saved the cost of the double windows by the difference in the coal burned before and after he had them.

During the coal strike some years ago, the following method of getting heat from cinders was evolved; it was given to me by one who had followed it for five years, but personally I know nothing of its efficacy. "Get ten-cents' worth of oxalic acid crystals and dissolve in two gallons of water with one bag of coarse salt. I got two bags for ten cents. (The price will be higher now.) Use one bag with a hod of fine ashes or cinders. Roll in balls and put in middle of fire-pot. It makes an exceedingly hot fire and is a great saving. I used three barrels of furnace cinders in one winter. If clinkers form, put into the fire the peeling of yellow turnips (rutabaga) and the clinkers drop off." The expense of trying this is not much and it may be found available for you.

For fuel save corn-cobs and dry them. Also the skins of vegetables if there is no other method of turning them to use. The writer once lived in a city where there was no coal to be had for three weeks, and the inhabitants used corn-cobs for fuel. They make an intense heat, soon over, and are not practical when one has other material but the cobs from corn eaten in summer time may be dried for kindling or for open fire in fall or winter.

Ice

It may seem impossible to go through a summer without ice and preserve butter, meats, and other foods, but thousands of persons in parts of the earth where artificial ice is not made and natural ice never forms do live comfortably without it. They have learned how to produce coolness by other means. Whatever method will keep heat in food can be modified to keep it cool; for instance, the fireless cooker, and the thermos bottle. Rapid evaporation is the explanation of some methods, keeping hot air from the foods to be cooled. The Department of Agriculture has prepared a bulletin giving directions for making an iceless refrigerator, and it is as useful in one State as in another, though it was written more particularly for those States with most heat and least convenience for getting ice. The Department of Publications will send the bulletin for ten cents. Meantime, try the suggestions to be given herein.

Never buy ice when it is cool enough to keep butter firm by putting it outside. If you want ice in really cold weather, all that you need do to get it is to set a pail or pan of water out-of-doors and let it remain there overnight. What need of paying the iceman for it?

Keep your provisions in the coolest place about the house. Keep butter and milk sweet without ice by placing in a pan, and this pan in another considerably larger. In the bigger one have enough water to come to the top of the smaller, and to the water add two tablespoonfuls of salt. Soak a large flowerpot until it is saturated with water. It must be large enough to go to the bottom of the larger pan, and to cover the smaller entirely when it is turned over it. Being porous, rapid evaporation is constantly going on, and will keep everything within firm and cool. A fancy flower-pot will not do for this. It must be the unvarnished terra-cotta pot. Once a week it should have another soaking. This is much the same as the method practised in some tropical countries to keep water cool, and is equally efficacious with foods.

Another adaptation of the same principle is to cover the inner dish with a towel which has been wet in cold water, folded in such a manner that the corners will hang down into the water of the large dish. Keep the pan in a cool place and butter will be as firm as in winter. By capillary attraction there will be a steady current of water from the dish through the cloth. Renew the water in the dish and change it daily. Campers often use this method of preserving perishable goods.

If you have occasion to save bits of ice in a room through the night, protect them by lining a dish with wet white flannel; fill it with ice, cover outside and in with more flannel, and set in a cool place. In a bowl the ice will last overnight. This is advantageous for an invalid.

If you take ice you can keep it in many ways from melting. The iceman says the best preservative is several thicknesses of newspaper over the ice. But if you feel a prejudice against having your ice thus protected you can try the pad described herewith. It is excellent in its effect. It must be kept as clean as the refrigerator should be. To make it, get a piece of heavy felting at least half an inch in thickness. Lay this between two sheets of woven wire, preferably the galvanized, as it will not rust and will last five times as long as the non-galvanized. Cut the three pieces an inch smaller on all sides than the cold chamber to permit free circulation of air. Dip the pad in cold water before placing it on the ice. As soon as the pad becomes damp from contact with the ice it throws out a blast of cold air which completely envelops the ice and makes it last much longer. The felt can be bought at a harness-maker's and the wire at any hardware store. The expense is trifling, and with good care the pad will last for years. It should be washed twice a week and sunned so that it does not become slimy from being wet.

Ice may be preserved also by fastening two sheets of cotton-batting between brown paper covers. Place under and over and around the sides. This keeps the ice, but encloses it so thoroughly that it does not cool the food chamber as well as the felting pad. A cover for a pitcher, like a tea cozy, that will completely enclose it, may be made of the cotton and brown paper, and the water or other fluid will remain cool a long time and the ice unmelted for hours. It is better as the cozy over a dish than as a pad for the ice chamber, but it is mentioned because it has merit and the first cost is less than that of the pad of felt and wire. In the long run it is more expensive, as the cotton pad is good only for the short time until it is flattened by the water and the paper is in bits, while the felt pad will last more than one season.

No one with any idea of thrift will leave ice standing by the door steadily melting in the hot air, thereby melting the money you have to pay for it. Rinse it at once and place in the chamber, covering it to keep it cool. If you take ice and yet wish to economize on it, never let your ice chamber get empty. Keep it full. It wastes less beside supplying more coolness. You do not get as much for your money with a ten-cent piece two days in succession as you do with twenty cents' worth every other day, though the actual outlay is the same. If you take larger pieces you will not need as many of them nor as much ice. Little pieces are wasteful because they so soon melt and leave the ice chamber getting warm again to melt the ice as soon as it touches the sides. Once filled, and the refrigerator well chilled, it can be kept thoroughly cool by small renewals and the box never allowed to become empty. Open the box once in a while to renew the air which becomes stale if unchanged.

If you find a hole in the ice-pan or the bottom of the refrigerator you can make it water-proof by a temporary mending with little labor and expense, but it will not be any protection against hot things. You do not put hot dishes in your refrigerator probably, at least you should not, so you can try this plan of mending it. Hold a paper under the hole. Melt paraffine, and while it is hot pour a coating over the hole, letting the paraffine run some inches beyond the hole. Some of the paraffine will run through the holes, which explains why the paper is held under. Make the coating of paraffine quite thick. Scrape off the part that ran through, as it is as good to use again. This repair work will serve as well for the purpose named as a piece of zinc soldered on, but will not last as long.

CHAPTER XII
POSSIBILITIES OF CORN MEAL

CHAPTER XII

POSSIBILITIES OF CORN MEAL

NEW ENGLAND owes its life to corn, for had its daily bread depended upon wheat in the early days when Puritans and Pilgrims were fighting their grim fight for existence there would have been no New England. Why may not these days of scarcity of wheat flour find profit from those when corn was the basis of bread food? No system of thrift goes far that does not recognize the benefits and economy of corn in the diet. Financially and hygienically corn deserves the old Indian name, "the friend of man."

Man might live many years on no other foods than corn and its products, which include oil, sugar, and molasses as well as meal. The yearly production of corn in this country is three times that of wheat, and the food value is greater than that.

Let your thrift begin with the greater use of corn meal to help out the contents of the flour barrel. Based on food value, corn is the leader in food, and at five cents a pound it is one of the cheapest in money. Whether served as hulled corn, hominy, grits, or some arrangement of meal, it is very nutritious and pleasant to the taste. When properly cooked it is easily digested, and its food value is rendered better for food by having bulk, as foods that do not have bulk are injurious to the system, which is so made that it must have something beside concentrated nourishment.

Corn meal at the time of writing this is five cents a pound; this amount of meal contains as much of food as ninety-one cents' worth of eggs at fifty cents a dozen, and fifty-six cents' worth of round steak at thirty cents a pound. Consider-

POSSIBILITIES OF CORN MEAL 189

ing these prices you will conclude that the high cost of living can be dealt an effective blow by taking corn meal for a weapon. It is an energy-making food.

Variety may be given to dishes of corn meal by adding dried or fresh fruits. The old time baked Indian pudding served by our grandmothers was one of the best of the corn-meal dishes. When there was not much else it was a dinner dish, and often it was the main dish at supper. It cannot be baked as it should be in a gas range because it needs slow cooking, and if baked in a gas-range oven it would not be an example of thrift, but it may be baked well in the fireless cooker. Here is a recipe for Indian pudding which is three generations old, and perhaps more. Heat a quart of milk and with it scald five tablespoonfuls of corn meal, stirring all the time. To these add one cup of molasses and a good-sized piece of butter, and bake in a deep dish for three hours or more with moderate heat. Stir several times when first set to baking to keep meal from settling. This was varied by the addition of peeled and quartered apples, was baked in an earthenware deep dish until it was a beautiful reddish brown that when turned out would stand quivering like a mold of jelly. It is the slow baking that produces such a result as that.

Such a pudding is all that any ordinary individual would need for a luncheon or supper, and is entirely too heavy for a dessert. As a one-dish meal it is delicious. It is to be eaten with cream.

Corn meal should have for cook one who likes it and is mistress over it, then from it such food will be made as will delight the appetite and preserve the health of the pocket-book.

Corn provides either alone or in combination with meat, milk, fish, or eggs, a one-dish meal which gives all the mate-

POSSIBILITIES OF CORN MEAL 191

rial the system requires at a meal of tissue-builders, starch, sugar, and fat. The fuel value or energy of corn meal to a pound is 1,795 calories, and in this respect corn stands above the other known cereals. The percentage of fat is greater than in other grains.

The simplest preparation of corn is hasty pudding, or mush, which is merely the meal dropped into boiling and salted water. With milk it forms a balanced dish, that is, it gives in proper proportion those chemical essentials which feed all parts of the body equally. It was the standard breakfast or supper dish of workers of two generations ago, and should be served occasionally by all those who want to make their money go to its full limit without taking proper sustenance from the family. The mush of old days was cooked all day, and was almost jellied when dished. All cereals are wholesomer for long-time cooking.

After the meal was stirred with a wooden, long-handled spoon until there were no lumps, it was set back on the stove to simmer all day, and it tasted like a different dish from the quickly made mush. After one meal as mush it was turned into a deep pan to cool. In the morning this was sliced and fried, and eaten with maple sirup, it was, and is, a food to be served in every family. The old way of frying was in shallow fat, but the modern way is to drop it in deep fat which is the less wasteful method. The Italians use mush with cheese and have a very nourishing food; as a meal it is better for having the addition of a green salad. The natives of Jamaica combine fish, lard, and corn meal. Note how these give the essentials of nutrition.

There is in Pennsylvania an organization of individuals, who once a year meet to eat scrapple and apple butter. Scrapple is a combination of meat and corn meal, usually spiced. Any kind of meat may be served in this way, but it is commonly pork. The mush is made in the proportion of one cup of meal to three and a half cups of water. It is always made and cooled in a pan like a bread-pan, then fried for breakfast. No extra fat is necessary.

Remains of fish from the day's dinner may be converted into fish-cakes by mixing with corn-meal mush in proportion of two cups of meal to one of fish, all held together by an egg. Season to taste. Bits of green peppers may be added if you like the flavor, or a few drops of onion juice.

Corn mush is very good with cheese for an addition, like the Italian polenta, and becomes a very hearty food. The sole accompaniment to these dishes of corn meal and meat, fish, or cheese is a green salad or tart fruits. Apples as sauce, salad, or baked are an appropriate side dish.

Apples are sometimes added to brown bread in small quantities. A cup of raisins to a loaf, or a cup of dates, pitted and quartered, are an improvement to brown bread, which of itself is a very satisfying meal, with butter. The following recipe for brown bread has passed from mother to daughter for four generations, and may be depended upon. One cup of corn meal, one of flour, one-half cup molasses, one of sour milk or water, teaspoonful of soda, one-half teaspoonful of salt. Steam three hours, with water boiling the first hour very fast, and do not let the water stop boiling, as if it does the bread will be heavy.

The Department of Agriculture supplies a bulletin on Uses of Corn Meal, to be had for the asking. It should be in every household, and followed by the home cook.

CHAPTER XIII

MEAT AND MEAT SUBSTITUTES

CHAPTER XIII

MEAT AND MEAT SUBSTITUTES

IF every family does without meat two days a week there will be a perceptible difference in the supply of meat in the market, and if no regulation is made obliging every one to go without on the same days, there will be no crowding of the markets some days and a corresponding lack on others. To go without meat is no hardship after one gets into the habit, and thousands live healthfully and contentedly without any meat day after day. They feel better without it. Eating is largely a matter of habit, in amount and in kind.

One of the largest sanitariums in the country is conducted without meat, neither officers nor patients ever eating flesh food, and there is no loss of energy from such abstinence. Meat is a stimulant, and only outdoor workers should eat it oftener than once a day. Autointoxication is caused by excessive meat-eating.

However, in spite of these facts most of the world will continue to crave the "flesh-pots of Egypt," and to desire to know how to make a little serve as more. Every housewife knows how hard it is in her small family to buy roasts to advantage and to use trimmings and bones. Instead of trying to use them before they spoil, can them. They may be canned as stock or as soup, and all the meat that one does not wish to eat can be canned by itself.

Simmer the bones for so long that every bit of meat will come off with scraping. Put them on with cold water and simmer so slowly that no rim of hardened albumen is around the top. Remove all the meat from bones, strain, and place the plain broth in jars, or to the stock add diced vegetables as for making vegetable soup, season, and sterilize as you do for other things you preserve in this manner. The principle of canning and the general process of canning are precisely the same, varying only in such minor details as sugar or no sugar, and so on.

The beef that has boiled from the bones may be seasoned and made into meatballs, to be cooked in bacon fat, which will add to its flavor. It has lost through simmering most of what flavor it had. It may be made into a nice baked hash with rice, potato, or such bread crumbs as one has, and a bit of onion and good seasoning.

The extra meat that has been cooked only once you can pack into jars, cutting the meat into bits so it will fit into the glass closely and be more open to the heat of sterilizing. Turn enough water into the jars to fill the interstices, and then boil with the top on, but not fastened down, until the middle pieces are thoroughly heated. Meat must cook a considerable time because the heat takes an hour or so to penetrate the inner pieces. Then, before removing from the boiling water, snap down the cover, and let the meat cool in the boiling water, as the water cools. Probably there will be some fat on the top. This is a preservative in itself. Beef, mutton, lamb, and veal have been canned in this way and I have never lost a jar. I do chicken or turkey in the same manner if there is any to do. There is every probability that the price of meat will go higher rather than lessen, and housewives do well to get into **the canning** habit, which is true thrift,—**making** the best and most of what they **have.**

If you have no ice and fear that meat will not keep, place it out-of-doors in a cool place so that the air can get at all sides of it. On the continent before the

War, many butchers had shops without ice. Sides of beef and pork hung by great hooks from the ceiling and all around them the air circulated day and night. At night it entered the shops through wrought-iron doors so that no stale air was retained in the shop, and the meat was as fresh and sweet as in any of the shops with which we are more familiar.

Here is a recipe for keeping meat that has been recommended by campers as reliable. Cover each piece of meat, chops, or roast with corn meal or oatmeal so thickly that it cannot come in contact with any other substance, and place in a current of air as cool as can be found. Do not wrap in paper, which will soon spoil meat under the best of conditions. I have been told that steak has been kept a fortnight in moderate weather and longer in cold, with no other protection than the wrapping of meal.

Once a delicious and expensive porterhouse when removed from the refrigerator indicated very unmistakably that it should have been cooked a day earlier. What was to be done? One does not willingly throw away such costly meat, and it seemed to be hopeless. This is what was done. The meat was scraped with a sharp knife until every sign of badness was removed from top, bottom, and fat. Then it smelled right, but to make certain, the meat was washed with saleratus water, and left in the water for ten minutes, and then wiped dry with cheese-cloth. Then it was wiped again with a clean dry cloth, and broiled. It was as sweet as ever it was, and very tender. This process is to be advised in every case when one has a doubt of the freshness of meat.

To preserve a ham, put it into a flour-sack, tie, and pack in a box of wood ashes. The lye that probably is in them will

MEAT AND MEAT SUBSTITUTES

keep it as sweet as you want it. For a ham that is to be used right along, keep in the flour-sack tied closely, and hang from hook in ceiling. A current of air is a preservative.

When you have not enough meat to make a dish of itself, use it as a flavoring. Take the odd ends of salt pork and bacon that are left after slicing and add them to peas or beans for soup. Or take them and add to a batter and bake as meat biscuits, or place a layer of rice, crumbs, or mashed potatoes, whichever you have, at the bottom of cups, and over that a layer of the minced meat, another layer like the first, wet it with water, stock, gravy, or tomato, whatever you have, and you will find the result when the contents of the cups are baked a very nice supper or breakfast dish. Use the bits of meat with greens or grind them and serve, dressed with a thick dressing, as salad or as filling for sandwiches.

Bacon rind fried out often returns a considerable amount of fat. Bits of bacon cooked or uncooked combine well with chicken, and a hash of bits of chicken, bacon, and potato is good enough for an epicure. Put all fragments of meat through the meat-grinder. Different meats may be used together. Add a little to a macaroni and tomato escallop. Even a tablespoonful will improve it. So will one sausage that you may have considered worthless. A spoonful of meat will improve a dish of hashed-brown potatoes or nearly any starchy food. It is not necessary to have enough meat for the combination to become a hash. Stuff tomatoes or green peppers with a bread-crumb dressing to which you have added even a very little bacon or ham, or any other meat. Meats of high flavor such as bacon, ham, and sausage add piquancy to more tasteless meats. These meats may be

MEAT AND MEAT SUBSTITUTES

added to a thick white or brown sauce, seasoned with mustard, and served very hot on toast. For sandwiches, add a little chopped pickle and dress with thick boiled dressing or mayonnaise. The result is not much like the ordinary sandwich with a slab of meat between slices of bread.

Have you a cupful of minced meat you do not know what to do with? Beside the ways to use it that have already been mentioned try this. Mix it with three good-sized mashed potatoes or the same amount in cold boiled rice. Add three well-beaten eggs, season and cook like an omelet, or bake in oven. Omelets may have a flavor from a spoonful of meat, and a slice of left-over liver cut in small pieces is very good. Any left-over meat may be potted by being rubbed smooth with butter or salad oil, seasoning well with mustard, salt, and cayenne or paprika. Ham thus treated is good enough to be prepared without any thought of saving. Meats potted will keep for some time in a cool place.

If you try to practise thrift by buying the cheaper cuts of meat there are two difficulties you are quite likely to meet. In the first place, you may not be able to find them, or any store that has shank of beef, flank, or such pieces. If the seller can dispose of the higher-priced cuts why should he take space for the lower-priced? That is the question once asked me. Many dealers do not intend to carry low-priced grades of meats. If they do not have them, generally the would-be buyer contents herself by getting the cuts she did not intend to buy, and the seller is that much ahead.

If you have been fortunate enough to buy as your good intentions prompted, perhaps you will feel that you were really a loser because the meat was tough and tasteless. That gives you your chance to show what good cooking will do. Long, slow cooking will make the toughest meat tender, and proper seasoning will give it savor. If to tough meat is added a spoonful of vinegar, or lemon juice, or if it is cooked with tomato it will become tender. The acid softens the fibre. I often add a spoonful of vinegar to the water in which I cook a fowl if it promises not to be tender.

To make meat savory let it lie overnight in a dressing of oil, vinegar, paprika, or onion juice, basting with the dressing, and the most tasteless meat will have a choice flavor and become tender. Never add salt to uncooked meat, as it toughens even tender meat. If you do not care to give the meat the bath of flavoring, season with herbs, or curry, but do not use the same flavoring every time. You can take the same cut and by varying the seasonings produce quite different results from it. A tasteless meat is changed and made appetizing by two or three strips of bacon added as basting for a roast when cooking.

An inexpensive English dish is lamb's heart stuffed with sage and onion. A heart is allowed for a person. They cost five cents apiece a short time ago. Each heart is carefully washed and trimmed. Then they are parboiled in hot water to which is added a spoonful of vinegar. After this they are stuffed with bread crumbs, to which onions and sage are added generously, with salt and pepper as liked. They are baked, base of heart down, and around the tiny pyramids may be placed the potatoes to bake in the pan. Baste often with water in which is a little fat. Baste potatoes as well as hearts, and they will become a beautiful brown. When hearts and potatoes are done, remove from the bake-pan and thicken the water with browned flour for gravy and you have the foundation of a nourishing and appetizing meal at small cost.

From a shin-bone, which is another inexpensive piece of meat, you may get a good deal at comparatively small cost. See that it has meat on it when you buy it. You can use the edge or aitchbone in the same way. Have the bone cracked, then put it to soak as for soup. Use cold water, let it come to the boiling point and then simmer. No meat should boil. Season with an onion, a clove, pepper and salt, and the ground celery tips you have dried. Use a tablespoonful to two quarts of water. When the soup has cooked down one-quarter, remove onion and meat and thicken the water with flour wet with cold water and stirred smooth. Be sure it is smooth or there will be lumps in the soup. Serve the soup with cubes of stale bread toasted. This gives one dish from the bone.

Take every bit of meat from the bone

and chop fine. Add to it a tablespoonful of crumbs, or as much more as the meat needs to take up the moisture. Season with onion, pepper and salt if needed, or with powdered poultry dressing. It is a combination of sage, thyme, marjoram and other flavors, and is much better than most cooks can prepare. Mix an egg into this and shape into balls. Brown in hot fat. Serve with tomato sauce if you wish them to be somewhat the nicer. The recipe for this is omitted as it is in all cook-books. Serve with this arrangement of meat any vegetable you fancy, and with a simple dessert you have a three-course dinner that has cost you little and is good enough to eat. You will be surprised to find how little your dinner will have cost you.

Another meat dish from the shin is spiced beef. Get quite a large weight, and have considerable bone, as the gelatine in it helps to make this dish better.

Have the bone well cracked. Put it to cook as directed above. Simmer until the meat can be pulled from the bone with a fork. Take from the water and remove all meat, chop it and the gristle fine, return to the kettle with cloves, allspice, bay leaf, herbs, mustard seed, and celery seed. Use a smaller proportion of the pungent spices and remember that cooking will intensify their strength. The meat is to be preserved by the spices. Cook the liquid down until very little is left. Turn the meat into a dish, a bread-tin is good, and let it stand until very cold. Slice and serve cold for supper or luncheon. Were this made of pork it would be the hog's-head cheese that our grandmothers kept regularly as part of the preparation for winter. If kept cool, it will keep a long time, thanks to the spices, or it may be put into a wide-mouthed crock, sterilized, covered with melted lard, and be kept indefinitely. Melted lard being somewhat expensive, you may substitute hot paraffine if you prefer. If this cheese is made in large quantity, it is better to prepare it for winter, but five pounds of the bone and meat will make a convenient dish to keep on hand in summer or winter. You can make up twenty pounds for winter.

The many ways in which you can vary your meat dishes number into the hundreds, and would make a fair-sized cookbook of themselves. If you wish to know more of them, experiment for yourself. The sole limitation on them is that the result shall taste "like more." Use your meat with rice, macaroni, potatoes, or other starches, with onions, carrots, beans, peas, turnips, tomatoes, and with combinations of these. You can scarcely fail to produce something good. Do not always work your ingredients into the same old stew. A good stew is a very

MEAT AND MEAT SUBSTITUTES 213

good thing, but nothing is good if one has a chance to get tired of it.

Boil sometimes, steam, broil, fry, and roast. Do not let anything come out greasy. It spoils the article and wastes a very important food product. A salad may be compounded occasionally, alone or with a vegetable, a very small amount of meat may be used for a hot sandwich if added to brown sauce, and by trying you will find yourself becoming more and more clever each month. It is very interesting to use your mind this way. It is also very profitable. Whatever you compound, you will have it good if it is not greasy and is well seasoned. "Well" does not mean highly, but to the proper taste.

The art of seasoning is that which makes French and Belgian cooks excel. The foundation materials are never better than what you have. Taine, himself a Frenchman who knew good cooking, wrote, "The table d'hôtes of Belgium are the best in the world." They are made so by the skill in seasoning. If you wish to equal their cooks, provide yourself with all the flavorings of which you hear and use them to give variety, not all at the same time. Do not scorn the effect of a single clove, or think it is too little to give a place. Try a bit of bay leaf— gather your bay while you are at the seashore and dry it for flavoring—and use it a little at a time. A well-flavored dish never has a strong taste of any one thing but a pleasant blending of many little things.

Thrift does not buy anything merely because it is cheap. One may have to buy that way or not buy at all, but thrift buys low-priced cuts and then makes them taste so good that one thinks them to have been high cost. If one has to throw away meat she has bought at a low price because it is unappetizing there is no thrift in it. There is no need for it.

The *ragouts* of the French are what we prepare from left-overs but they are not served as any makeshift but as something really good, and they are. So may be your dish from flank, or shin, or neck, or any tough bit. You will have a pride in developing your talent for making good things at low cost that you never had in any other accomplishment, and you will have a happy home. The woman who is a good and economical cook usually has a home one likes to stay in.

You will find it a pleasant change from meat to have fish twice a week, and somewhat more profitable in money. It is by no means a poor exchange. From fish you may have soup, chowder, stew, bake, roast, fry, boil, broil, salad, escallop, fish-cakes, fish-pie, fish-pudding, and hash. Any article that offers such a range is worth your consideration. Freshen salt fish in sour milk, laying the fish back up in the dish. Some fish are comparatively tasteless, and to such you may give flavor by leaving in the bath of lemon juice or vinegar with onion or other seasoning, with or without oil according to the nature of the fish, if it is dry flesh or fat. Or you can give flavor to your fish after it is cooked by serving with sauce *tartare*, a mayonnaise to which is added enough mustard and paprika with a bit of minced pickle to bite the tongue. Or you have the choice of several other sauces.

It is a good plan to serve with fish such vegetables as have a distinct flavor, as peppers, cucumbers, cabbage salad, beets, carrots, and onions. A boiled fish is distinctly a different dish if the water in which it cooks has in it a little celery seed or dried and ground celery tops, a clove and a peppercorn or two. A dry fish, one with little natural oil, should be baked with slices of bacon to baste it, or slices of fat pork, which are equally good, and cheaper.

Massachusetts would scarcely have come to its present estate if in earlier days it had not been held by the cod dignified now in that State as "The sacred codfish." What it was to the earlier settlers of Plymouth Bay Colony it can be to-day to others, for it is one of the cheapest and best of fish, either fresh or salted. Fresh cod may be baked, broiled, or fried, and is made into a delicious fish chowder. A fresh cod salted to stand overnight, in the morning wiped free from salt, placed on a bake-sheet, put into hot oven, baked very quickly, and dressed with butter and slices of lemon is very well worth eating. It may be dressed with strips of bacon before baking if one wants a change from butter.

Small fish may be baked in a bean-pot or casserole to be eaten hot or cold and will be good for a long time if kept in a cool place. To prepare them, place a layer of cleaned fish on the bottom of the pot, scatter whole cloves over the top, mixed with peppercorns and mustard seed, add another layer of fish, and then spice, until the dish is filled. Have spice on the top, and use discretion in scattering over the top of the fishes. Cover the fish with a mixture of vinegar and water, twice as much vinegar as water, and bake slowly until the liquid is well absorbed. All bones will be so softened by the acid that they will give no trouble to the eater. This is a satisfactory method of laying by any extra fish. Larger fish may be cut in sections and treated in the same manner. It is a good thing to have in the house when emergencies arise and one cannot go to the market. Fish may be potted by the rule given for potting meat, but bones must be removed and great care taken that no bits of bone remain in the paste.

Left-over fish is a good foundation for a salad, or it may be warmed up in an egg sauce, which is drawn butter or white sauce with egg added. Egg sauce is the proper accompaniment for a boiled fish and the left-over of sauce and fish may be made into a scallop with potato or crumbs, and baked until brown. The sauce should be the top. If it is a little less than the amount needed, you can fill up with milk. The effect is pleasing if over the last layer of sauce you spread a few fine crumbs. Everything in this being cooked, not more than fifteen minutes in a hot oven will be required for its baking.

"I don't like fish" will not be heard in your family if you know how to cook it, and that knowledge is a part of thrift. Those who go camping near the ocean or inland lakes find that fish is a very good thing to eat, and they will like it if the cook learns how to prepare it so that it has flavor. Bacon is an excellent fat to use in nearly all ways of cooking fish except the few oily kinds. It has so distinct a flavor that it improves most. Salt fat pork fried crisp was a favorite part of a codfish dinner in New England before its people became so prosperous that they ceased to economize. The fish was stripped into bits as small as they could be pulled, freshened by having boiling water poured over it several times. If fish stands in water and boils up much it toughens, but if soaked or scalded in three or four waters it is tender. The pork was cut in inch pieces very thin, and fried out. It was perfectly crisp and the fat was a dressing for the fish and the baked potatoes which went with the dinner. In the land of the codfish, beets and carrots always are served with the fish and potatoes.

The Fish Commission of the United States has done a wonderful but little-known work (so far as the public is concerned) in introducing new fish to the people. The fish supply of this country is enough to feed the inhabitants for a long time and negatives any probability of starvation though there become a greater shortage of meat than is at all likely. Not only have new varieties of food fish been discovered, but a wide range of methods of cooking them have been developed, and this information is practically free to any housewife who wishes it enough to send to the Fisheries Department at Washington for it. At the outside, the bulletins will not cost over five or ten cents and they give careful directions for cooking fish in many inviting guises. Eat more fish and the meat problem will cease to be a problem. The health will be improved, and the pocket-book will have something always in it, if you want it to have.

Thrift influences you to make the

most of the possibilities that are at your hand, and you want to make sure that you are doing this before you groan too much over the high cost of living. Perhaps that bugbear is made stronger by lack of knowledge how to use what you have. In the days when the cost of living was lower there were fewer kinds of foods and the average family ate dishes that only the poorest eat now, codfish for instance with pork scraps, and stews for supper. While you need not do that to be thrifty, you will find you can make your money buy to better advantage by knowing more about foods, and what you can make with what you can command of materials within your financial reach. Learn that and you will become past-mistress of thrift, and independent.

Try a Welsh rabbit some time for the main dish of a luncheon. It is much more than a light dish for a pleasure time. It

MEAT AND MEAT SUBSTITUTES

is a hearty dish and a valuable meat substitute. You should not serve potatoes or rice with it, but turn it on toast, and have with it a salad of green vegetables. If you have any of the rabbit left do not discard it. Spread saltines or soda crackers with the mixture, brown in the oven, cool, and wrap in waxed paper and you will have excellent cheese-crackers that will keep as well as those bought in boxes, provided they are hidden. They are rich in food value and may be added to a meatless meal. Do not serve any other cheese preparation with them.

Peanuts deserve a larger place in the household dietary. There is enough nourishment in a pint of peanuts for a meal for a hearty, out-of-doors worker, and if eaten with some less concentrated food might be chosen once in a while in place of meat.

Peanuts may be cooked very much like beans, and when baked are very good.

For a peanut roast, grind the nuts very fine, mix with bread crumbs, and hold together with beaten egg. Season to taste, and bake until brown. One may have peanut soup, peanut roast, peanut salad, peanut butter sandwiches, peanut cakes, and thus have a peanut meal if one chooses it. Brown bread is much the best for the peanut-butter sandwiches.

CHAPTER XIV

DESSERTS

CHAPTER XIV

DESSERTS

I COUNT it wise to have desserts for dinner even if one is trying to save to the last penny. They add to the meal certain elements that the system craves, and which are well supplied as dessert, and they make a pleasant finish to the meal. Where children are they help to form the manners of the well-bred individual, and if the only dessert is a bread and sugar sandwich, served on a pretty plate, with the dishes of the previous course removed, it has helped the child toward gracious manner to have it given him. Having this conviction, I should always have something for dessert, however simple it might be.

As a rule, desserts should be very light,

but this may vary according to the food of the earlier part of the meal. In the usual household there are only two courses at dinner, the heavy or meat course and the dessert. Economy really would be better served by having three, soup, meat or its equivalent, and dessert, for no more food would be eaten, and the soup is better in most cases for the individual than more heavy food. Three courses would be a factor for helping out with the meat problem in the ordinary home.

If the first part of the meal is meatless and rather light, the sustenance needed may be gained by a heartier dessert such as a pie or pudding. We know of course that pies have had much said against them by dietists, but if dangerous, they are so slow a poison and so good—if good at all—that most of us will continue to take some chances on them. As a general statement, it may be said that fruit

DESSERTS

desserts are better than pies or puddings except in cold weather, when the fuel value of the latter makes them to be liked more than the lighter food.

Any canned or fresh fruit makes a tempting dessert if served with a spoonful of whipped cream on it, and a little cream is not as expensive or as thriftless as you may think. It is one of the best of foods. Fruit may have a meringue of white of egg whipped to a froth with a spoonful of sugar, or it may be served in its original condition.

Any fruit whip may be made by mashing the fruit, uncooked if soft enough to whip, and cooked if hard like apple, beating it with the egg-beater with the addition of sugar as needed. Serve in glasses. It is as pretty as it is good. You may add a bit of whipped cream to that for looks. Cream whipped will "go" nearly three times as far with a dessert as it will if served unwhipped.

You may make three desserts from your fruit whip, first as it is just made, then with the cream, and lastly, you may place it upon rounds of buttered toast, or slices of stale cake or cottage pudding.

Boiled rice shaped into forms, crowned with fruit, and served with sugar and milk, will please children and adults. Teacups may be used if you have no regular molds. Make a food attractive to the eyes and children will enjoy what otherwise they will refuse to eat. You can hollow out the top of the rice and drop a cherry in the hollow and that pleases the child. A delicious and very inexpensive pudding is made of rice in the following way: Into the baking-dish in which the pudding will be served (butter well) turn a quart of milk; add three heaping tablespoonfuls of rice and the same amount of sugar. Stir when placed in the oven and continue to stir until rice is swollen. Season as you like it. Add raisins if you wish, but they are not needed for excellence. Put into a good oven, but as soon as the milk has become thoroughly hot lessen the heat of the oven as the deliciousness of this pudding depends upon slow baking. It should bake slowly for three hours and the milk never bubble. This pudding is to be eaten cold, and it will seem like a jelly.

From biscuit dough you may have a wide range of desserts; cut in biscuit rounds, bake, split, and fill with fruit: there is the individual shortcake. You may make a filling of raisins and dates or raisins only, and you may cook the fruit, one cup to one-half cup of water, one-half cup of sugar, and when thick turn over it the beaten white of an egg. You can make this filling for the biscuit shortcakes or for a layer cake in which you will use the yoke of the egg.

Instead of cutting the dough, roll it

very thin and spread with cinnamon and sugar. Roll like a jelly cake, and from the end of the roll cut in inch wide slices. Bake in a quick oven, laying each slice flat on the bake-tin. With a cup of coffee these are nice for dessert or for afternoon tea. Now you can roll the dough thin for another dessert, but this time you will not cut it. You will spread it with some jelly that did not thicken well when you made it. Then start at the smallest end and roll to the other side. Bake this roly-poly and you will find it good. If you have no jelly you can spread it with nuts and raisins run through the finest grinder, or slices of fruit, sweetened as needed. The fruit must be sliced very thin and the dough must be so thin that when rolled it has a chance to bake through. The thicker the roll, the slower must be the oven, otherwise the outside will be burned before the inside is baked. Practise makes perfect, and is the only thing that does make perfect the rolling of these bread-dough desserts, but they are worth the effort. When you have the knack you can experiment and find something else that rewards your efforts.

In England, griddle-cakes are served as dessert. They are the thinnest cakes imaginable, are rolled like jelly-cakes after being spread with sugar or jelly, and eaten without any other accompaniment.

At least once a week a tapioca dessert should be served in a family where there are children. It is not only very good but it is one of the least expensive of foods. Tapioca is excellent for little folk and they always like tapioca desserts. In cooking it, remember that it stiffens considerably as it cools and is usually eaten cold. You can give great variety to the dessert of tapioca, and if you wish to make it more of a food you can use milk and eggs in the composition of your dessert, but you can have many delicious puddings without either.

The old-fashioned tapioca required overnight soaking, but the present can be used without preliminary soaking, which is a great convenience. You can modify the following recipe in many ways by changing the fruit and with each you will like it. Drain a can of peaches or use the equivalent amount of the fresh fruit. To peach syrup add enough boiling water to make three cups of liquid. Heat to boiling point and add tapioca, prepared according to directions on package. These directions vary with different makers. Add three-fourths cup of sugar; cook in double-boiler until transparent. Line a pudding-dish with peaches cut in quarters, turn the tapioca over them, and bake in moderate oven. Apples cooked in this manner are delicious.

Tapioca pudding may be made with coffee, chocolate, jelly, or any fruit juice, and the making is simple. Two tablespoonfuls of tapioca, a scant quart of boiling water, three tablespoonfuls of sugar, make ample dessert for four persons, in the form of either baked or boiled pudding. If a coffee tapioca is made, use the hot coffee left from breakfast in place of water, and do the same with chocolate. Treat as in the recipe given above. Instead of baking, after the tapioca has boiled to transparency add the fruit and cook until it is soft. It is equally good.

Corn-starch is also the base of many good simple desserts, but they do not quite equal those from tapioca. The suggestions given for tapioca are as good for corn-starch, and with either it is better to have the pudding too soft than too stiff. When it is too stiff it makes one think of paste, which is not appetizing. Banana or orange is a pleasant addition to either and at little cost. One banana will flavor the pudding, but two oranges are needed for an orange pudding.

Corn-starch may be the foundation for blanc-mange, and an economical dessert is cocoanut blanc-mange. Save enough milk from a quart to mix with the corn-starch and cocoanut, a little more than a cupful, and put the remainder into a double-boiler to heat. When the milk is hot, add a quarter-cup of dessicated cocoanut and five level tablespoonfuls of corn-starch rubbed smooth with cold milk, cook until smooth and done. Sweeten with two tablespoonfuls of sugar, and turn the whole into molds. Set where they will be cold, and when serving sprinkle with shredded cocoanut. Puddings will not stick to molds that have been wet and are well chilled when the contents are added.

Junket tablets and Irish moss combined with milk make desirable desserts.

Rules for junket are printed with the tablets. Irish moss is tied in muslin, boiled with milk, and is the original blanc-mange. It may be found by the sea on the Atlantic coast, or bought from the druggist.

Eggless puddings for cold days often make a finish to a dinner that pleases a man more than any fancy dish, however nice it may be, and bring a satisfaction a lighter dessert fails to give in winter. When you want a pudding that supplies nearly as much food as meat try this suet pudding. Two cups chopped suet (if it mats as you chop, sprinkle it with flour). Two-thirds of a cup of molasses, a cup of sweet milk, a teaspoonful of soda, four cups of flour, a cup of chopped raisins. Mix and steam four hours. Season with spices if liked. This is better on reheating than at first.

Graham steamed pudding is better than you might think it would be. For it take two cups of Graham flour, cup of molasses, cup sweet milk, cup of raisins, teaspoonful soda and a little salt. Steam this pudding two and a half hours.

The nicest and whitest of the eggless puddings is cranberry pudding. Take a cup of sugar, a cup of milk, two cups of flour, three tablespoonfuls melted shortening—if you use a cooking oil for shortening take only a spoonful—two teaspoonfuls baking-powder, a coffee-cup of cranberries. This is very light and good. Substitute raisins for cranberries if you wish, and lessen the sugar one-half, or use dates, or both. Fresh berries make a good addition, but the dough must be made stiffer to balance the moisture of the berries. Use for any of these the pudding-sauce you prefer. Bake this pudding.

Apples furnish material for many inviting and inexpensive desserts. Bake them after they have been cored and stuffed with raisins and nuts. Serve with cream. Any cook-book will give you hints for using apples and making desserts to be enjoyed. Take slices of stale bread, butter them, and place in a bake-dish in which they will be served. Sprinkle them lightly with sugar, and over each layer of bread put apple-sauce generously. If it is moist, nothing more will be necessary, but if the sauce is dry, turn enough milk over it to moisten it. Bake until it is done, and eat with milk and sugar or with hard sauce. These are simply hints for help in devising simple desserts. It is safe to substitute one fruit for another, and to experiment with what you have, using your judgment for such changes as should be made.

When you have tired of prunes in their usual form, pit them and add to a custard, or reheat them with some minced lemon or orange-peel added to the water in which you heat them. This makes them into quite a different dish. Add quartered prunes to a lemon jelly; for breakfast or dessert, try a combination of prunes cut in half with segments of orange added. Uncooked prunes, pitted and each stuffed with a nut-meat or raisin, make a good and cheap dessert. Peanuts may be chosen, and peanuts are a true food.

Any dish compounded largely with milk will be nourishing. Milk is one of the best of foods, and those who cannot eat it cold or uncooked can generally eat it in soup or other cooked forms. Let it serve in that way if there are children in the family. A simple milk dish is made by adding milk to crackers. If you can get the old-fashioned kind that splits in halves, take them. Split, butter, place in pan, and add milk to cover. Season with salt only. Bake slowly until the milk is entirely absorbed and the crackers more than doubled in size. This may be elaborated by adding an egg, well beaten, to the milk before covering the crackers, or it may have slices of apple or other uncooked fruit or raisins and prunes, and in that case add sugar as needed. It is good as a simple dessert or as a breakfast dish.

CHAPTER XV
THRIFT AND TEXTILES

CHAPTER XV

THRIFT AND TEXTILES

BUYING covers all needs of the family, and though the wastes are more numerous in the kitchen than in any other department of the household, it is equally necessary to look after leakages in buying wearing-apparel, household linen, and all such supplies. In these the best is the cheapest, but it is not always true that the highest-priced is the best. The highest-priced are novelties which have no merit above older patterns except that of novelty—if such it be. For service in the household, a design that is ten years old in table-linen, sheeting, towels, and such things is just as good as the latest and will cost one-third less at times. It is thrift to renew these things when the yearly sales are closing out the novelties that came in the previous season. One can buy better at the sales than at other times, and it is distinctly thrifty to satisfy one's needs for the year then.

Thrift does not wait until everything has been worn thin before buying new, but gets a few things as the year goes by. It costs much more to make good the neglect of several years than to foresee the wear and to replenish as one knows wear is telling on household linen. A pair of sheets and pillow slips, a few towels, et cetera, make no great drain on the family treasury, while buying them in quantity does. It is easier to find five dollars a year than to wait and have to pay twenty-five.

If you do not feel that you can afford to buy fine table-linen it is not necessary to economize by using table oilcloth. There are as pretty designs in mercerized cotton as one need want to see and at much less cost than for linen. With these you can keep a table that you need not be ashamed of. Treat yourself to one fine linen cloth for the festal occasions of the family, birthdays, Christmas, and special guests, but use for every day the napkins and cloths that you can afford, and keep your table clean and charming. You can do that even if dollars are very few. Pretty dishes are not costly and soap and water will keep cloths clean. For breakfast and supper let doilies take the place of the long cloth. It saves work and is much more attractive and is also the favored way at the present day. It is poor thrift that expresses itself in soiled table furnishings.

The table and its supplies are the heart of the home, the expression of its highest attainment in fineness of living, and for the sake of all who gather about it let it be as perfect as your means can buy, not so much in high cost of cloth and food as in cleanness, smoothness of the cloth, and the manners of your family. It is better to have only bread and butter served with the courtesy that is the charm of personal intercourse than untidy abundance and the personal bearing that corresponds.

The table is one place where one may not choose what is easier if one does her duty to her children, because the fineness of the child's nature and his future outlook are affected by the table training he receives. One may have the manner that a prince is supposed to have if from early childhood he has lived graciously, for it costs nothing in money to have the grace of the well-bred, but it takes thought, and constant attention. Let your child have the simplest food—he will be the better for it—but do not use economy on anything that will make it possible for him to grow up with an idea that he can eat with his fingers, or on a cracked dish at a coverless table or one with a dirty cloth.

Treat children as you wish them to be when the days of childhood are past. If you can do it for no other reason, do it because it is an asset in business that increases in value as business demands become more intensive. The day of the successful boor is nearly at its end. "Politeness is surface Christianity," wrote Dr. Oliver Wendell Holmes. It is the finest thrift, the farthest-reaching, to insure its being a part of your children. Those who have learned in childhood the niceties of conduct will not forget them under the most primitive conditions. They are a part of the individual like his morals, but those who get their good breeding after adult years have come to them revert to the habits of childhood at every opportunity and often without knowledge of doing so. Keep the table looking as it should even if the children wear patches. There is no disgrace in patches but there is nothing else than disgrace in bad manners.

Now let us return to the point of digression. The rules of buying are in general the same; the principles of thrift in the kitchen will be the same in the parlor or the bedroom.

Buy the standards in quantity if thereby you get reduction in price, if not, you would better save your money until the need comes and have the interest on it. Never buy anything for which you have not a real need. If you can buy sheeting very cheaply at a certain time and you are near the time when sheets must be bought you do well to get them, but buying what is not needed is a snare and a delusion that takes many good dollars out of some pockets.

If your time has a marketable value or if you are not able to sew you will find it more economical to buy your garments ready-made. A dress can be bought that looks well and will be fitted to you properly for much less than the same garment can be made, but not for as little as you can make it if you know how to sew. If every girl would take a course of instruction in dressmaking and millinery she would save herself many dollars and dress herself better than she ever did before, while spending no more, and very likely less. She would also have a business, whether she ever followed it or not, in which a really good worker is never without profitable employment.

If one has a good dress that is worth making over it pays her to have a dressmaker at home. Never hire a poor dressmaker, for she will spend half her time correcting the mistakes she makes in the other half.

Because they are wasteful, the thrifty will not buy mixtures of cotton and wool. They do not wear alike, and they shrink surprisingly. All materials about the unshrinking quality of which there is a doubt should be shrunken before they are made up. Men's trousers should not be bought without a guarantee that they will not shrink. It is distinctly poor economy to buy garments without such warrant of good material. More than one man whose dollars are limited has bought clothing at what he considered a bargain, only to find after being out in a rain that he could no longer wear what he had bought. That kind of buying is extravagance at any price, as any worthless thing is. No woolen clothing to-day can be sold at a low price, for wool is scarce and therefore dear.

Men's clothing may be found ready-made, following good lines, and men wear ready-made garments without the sense of being ill dressed that once was taken for granted with such clothing. Just as the home-made shirt is practically unknown, and the custom-made seldom worn, so now the entire wear of a man is ready for him to don when minor corrections have fitted it to his figure. The same is becoming so much the case with women's garments that it is really an economy for the woman, whose time or strength is limited, to get ready-made gowns from a good house. She will have them fitted to her, and the saving of time and bother is a relief.

Whether it is cheaper to have a good dressmaker come to the house, or take material to her to make, or to buy ready-made, are questions that have been debated much. It is cheaper to buy a dress ready-made than to buy the same materials and take them to a dressmaker, counting in dollars and cents. There are, however, times when there is no question that it pays to have a good woman, skilful with her needle, work at your home. Turn it into an arithmetical problem and you will find your answer. Here is a dress that with a little revision will do good service for a season and save the expense of another. If that revision costs less than the new one would cost, it pays to have it made. Into the cost you must reckon the dinner of the seamstress. There is no profit in hiring a workwoman who makes mistakes. There is better profit in hiring one who charges more but is so competent that each stitch is right, each line of the shears just as it should be. The profit or loss in hiring work done at home depends upon the personal equation, which each must know for herself better than it can be told by another.

In the ordinary household it is thrift to buy one's sheeting by the quantity and make one's sheets on the machine. It is folly to hem them by hand. One gets a much better sheet for the same money by making it herself. Life is too short and too full to put any great amount of it into hemming ordinary things by hand.

Another point to consider in buying is to get that which accords with your income and position in life. If your income warrants paying for good silk and you want it, buy it, but if you cannot pay for good silk do not be guilty of the waste and sham of buying a poor quality. Things that should be expensive look the cheapest and commonest of everything when bought in imitation or in cheap quality, and are really very dear because they do not last.

Cloth at fifty cents a yard which is so mixed with cotton that it looks well only three months is higher in price than material at a dollar and a half that will wear two years and look well longer when remade.

Silk stockings at fifty cents do not look well on any one. They are shabbier than good cotton ones and much dearer at the same money. A fine hose at fifty cents really looks better and will outwear four pair of cheap, and cheap-looking silk at the same price. No girl on a salary of ten dollars a week is well-dressed if she wears silk stockings at any price, or if a gift. She is attempting to be what she is not, which is not good taste. If women could realize that imitations make one look ill-dressed, and be content to clothe themselves truthfully they would serve the gods of propriety, thrift, and beauty instead of those to whom belong waste and vulgarity. "Simplicity is the highest art," and it is a characteristic of genuineness.

CHAPTER XVI
CARE OF CLOTHING

CHAPTER XVI

CARE OF CLOTHING

Care of clothing is true thrift, and more important to one who would look well on a small amount than the original buying, for it not only doubles the life of a garment but keeps it looking well as long as anything of it is left. This is noticeably true of material of good value. With cheap garments, good care is more necessary if one is to have any satisfaction whatever from them.

Nothing looks well when there are spots to be seen on it, so keep on hand always ready for use a good cleansing preparation. An application will remove the spot before it has become hard. Try the following, adding one and a half ounces of pure white soap to a pint of boiling water. Shave the soap so that it will more quickly dissolve. Boil for ten minutes after the soap has dissolved, and then turn into a glass or china holder. Keep closely covered. This was recommended to me as being equal to the needs of the family from taking out ink-spots to cleansing gloves.

Fresh ink-spots may be removed by soaking in milk. Old ink-stains that have been dried in may be taken out by washing in hot lard. Wash just as one would with water, and wash again and again, finally washing out the lard in soapy water. I have known this to work wonders with a bed-cover on which an ink-bottle had been upset.

Paint on clothing should be treated with turpentine and ammonia in equal parts. Saturate two or three times if necessary and wash out in white soap-suds.

A mixture of Fuller's earth and powdered alum, equal parts, is said to be

CARE OF CLOTHING

excellent for cleaning white suède gloves. For the glacé kid give different treatment. Undressed kid may also be cleaned by rubbing with the finest sandpaper. It should not be scrubbed but lightly rubbed. The effect is excellent. These are better than gasoline for cleaning because they leave no odor. The paste first mentioned will clean glacé gloves.

Clear, black coffee diluted with water and containing a little ammonia may be used for cleaning black cloth garments. To renew thin black dresses, dip a cloth in gum-arabic water—quite a weak solution—and lay over the cloth on an ironing-board covered with black. Use a black cloth to dip in the solution. Pin the cloth smoothly to the board, right-side down. Cover with the cloth that was dipped. Over this have a dry piece, and press with a hot iron. The effect is very good. If you wish to treat a white muslin use rice-water instead of

the gum arabic but pin it to the c
cover with the wet cloth and the dɪ
you did for the black muslin. It
look like new. Never wring any
material. Pat it dry enough to p
wrong-side up.

If you wish to remake a dress, r
carefully and pull out all the thre
Take a good day for cleaning it and
ready a bath of soap bark. Five c
worth from the druggist will give
all you need. Put the dry bark
cheese-cloth bag and pour over it a ga
of boiling water. Let the decoction s
until dark colored. Put in a tub or
with your goods with warm wate
cover them and let stand overnight.
the morning souse up and down,
rinse thoroughly with warm water.
not wring. Hang in a shady place ɪ
dry, or nearly dry, and if it has not c
smooth press it under a clean cloth
a hot iron. This treatment is like m

for removing spots and can be used on material of delicate colors without harming them in the least. There are women who clean their woolen coats and dresses in this manner without ripping them, but that requires some expertness as it does to wash them in gasoline.

A gasoline bath can be used for laces, dainty wraps, and nearly anything, though since the price of that cleanser has risen so much it is about as cheap to send them to a professional. A bath of gasoline means three relays of it. In the first the material soaks enough to loosen the dirt, and in the other two it is rinsed out. The cleanest things are first treated and the " waters " are used until they are dirty. No water must touch the garments. The cleaning must be done out-of-doors because gasoline is dangerous to handle in a house. I have a friend who cleans feathers, hose, gloves, and various little things including summer frocks that do not launder well in water. They need no ironing when gasoline-cleaned. Personally, my experience has never been successful in the use of gasoline. If I try to take out a spot with it, a bigger one comes in the place of what I tried to remove, but the fault is personal, not in the method which many follow regularly.

Gloves may be cleaned with gasoline by the most inexpert if she will do it this way. Put the gloves in a quart glass jar. Several pairs may be done at one time. There must be gasoline to cover them but not to fill the jar. Let them stand half an hour, then shake the jar fast. The dirt will fall out of the gloves. Remove lid of jar and put the gloves into another with an equal amount of gasoline. Shake in this, and if after standing ten minutes and the shaking they are not clean, give them another bath in a third jar. That will make them as clean as ever they can be made.

To do one pair of gloves this way is extravagant, but the gasoline for one pair may be used to clean a dozen pairs and its price then is not excessive for the return.

If you have a nice dress which has been spotted with something that you are not sure of, do not try to remove it. Send it to a professional cleaner. Removing stains is a regular business and wonders can be wrought by one who knows it. Never practise on expensive articles. It is cheaper to entrust the work to one who knows just what to do and how it should be done.

One of the most profitable forms of thrift is to have street gowns for the street only, removing as soon as one gets home. Nothing can demoralize a gown more than lounging around in it, or wearing it out about the kitchen when preparing supper or dinner. Have a well-made street dress of good material, remove it as soon as you get home, and substitute a pretty house gown that you can make for yourself by the help of any dependable pattern. By house dress I mean one that is daintier than is permissible for street wear. Under the term house dress is not included kimonos, wrappers, or any of the sloppy things that are discreditable to a woman in her home and enough to make matrimony seem a failure to any husband. Even in these days of high prices it is possible to find material as low as a quarter of a dollar a yard from which a woman can construct attractive house frocks which will make her look pleasant to the eyes of her family, and her world will be happy. A well-fitted and well-made calico house gown better becomes a woman than a kimono of silk when occupied with her duties, and far better than a dirty, spotted woolen which can no longer be worn on the street.

CARE OF CLOTHING

Clothing for man, woman, and child should be hung on hangers as soon as taken off. It should be aired before being shut in a closet. All articles should be dusted before being put away, should have the needed stitches taken, or laces freshened up, and everything done that should be before it is worn again. One's clothing should be kept in condition for wearing, not left neglected until time to wear it again. Care will keep it young in appearance much longer than is otherwise possible.

If you have a dress of good material which has faded, or if you are tired of its color, why not dye it? If you are afraid to try it yourself, have it done by a good dyer. It is not necessary to rip anything to have it dyed. If an overcoat is of all-wool and has become shabby from wear it may be made to look well by a good dyer's work on it, and save the expense of a new one.

Cottons that have become streaky have been dyed so that they looked prettier than new. I know a very charming frock now pale green which began as a lavender crêpe, faded until it looked more like a rag than anything else. The owner boiled it in cream-of-tartar water and made it white, then dyed it, changed the neck, added touches of black velvet, and at the cost of a few cents had a dress that has been greatly admired. Had it not been dyed it would have been worthless. She made it herself. It does not often pay to hire such work done.

Shoes are so expensive that one likes to know how to make them last their longest. Two pairs worn alternately will last nearly as long as three pairs, each worn regularly until beyond repair. When the shoes are removed from the feet, every trace of dust should be wiped from them, an old stocking-top being excellent for this purpose. Always air a

CARE OF CLOTHING

shoe before setting it in a closed place. Keep strings or buttons in order, and to do this have extra strings and buttons at hand.

Vaseline with lampblack added makes a good dressing for shoes, and well rubbed, will make a shine. The oil preserves the shoe and should be rubbed enough to soften it. Vaseline must not be used on light shoes because any oil deepens the color.

If shoes have been wet until they are soaked, the stiffness may be avoided by stuffing them while wet with newspaper rolled in little balls. Fill the shoes, stuffing the balls into the toes, and filling out the shape as if the foot were in the shoe. The leather will be pliable when dry. It is not wise to set wet shoes in a hot place to dry. Sometimes that treatment ruins them. Shoes filled with oats will keep their proper shape, but to use oats in that fashion to accomplish an end served as well by old papers is not thrift. All articles of leather which have become too stiff for use through being wet may be softened by vigorous rubbing with kerosene.

Corn meal is a very good cleaner. I have used it to clean flannel collars and cuffs, and it serves for many other things. It is fine for taking dust from straw hats, and whitens when used with lemon juice. It is to be sprinkled on and rubbed in with a brush. Any light straw may be cleaned with a solution of oxalic acid, rubbing it in with a small brush. The solution should be made of an ounce of the crystals to a quart of water. See that the hat dries in the shape wanted. For ten cents a Panama hat can be cleaned to look like new. Mix equal parts of oxalic acid and precipitated sulphur. Dissolve half a teaspoonful in half a tumbler of cold water, remembering that you are dealing with

CARE OF CLOTHING

a deadly poison when you use oxalic acid, and must be very careful where you put it and how you use it. Dip a clean sponge in the liquid and wipe the hat until clean. Dry in the sun and the hat will reward you by its appearance.

If hats instead of being dirty are discolored by the sun, they can be bleached with sulphur fumes. Country girls sometimes braid the straw for their hats and then bleach the straw or the completed hats by hanging to the bottom of a barrel which is turned upside down over a fire-smudge sprinkled with sulphur. This is a successful method of bleaching, practicable only when one has outdoor space. Sulphur fumes are unsafe in enclosed spaces.

Faded hats can be colored with dyes that come for hats. Sometimes they are not fast colors and then as soon as a rain comes the result is very unpleasant, but others are rain-proof and will improve the hat greatly. You remember how one of the "Little Women" painted her hat? There is no patent on the idea and any one who wants to try it can do so. Dyes for hat-coloring are low-priced and of many tints, so it is quite possible to turn even a sailor old friend into a new one.

Laces also may be dyed to match a costume if one cares for that trimming. An old waist was metamorphosed into a beautiful new one by being dyed brown, with lace to match and only such changes made in it as mode of sleeve necessitated. Thrift will lead women to-day to look over the put-away garments and revive for wear those that may be done over by any of these suggestions.

Pack away all garments where they shall have no chance to get dusty. Wrap silks and ribbons in blue paper and then in brown. There is a tinge of chloride of lime in white paper and that will discolor them. Packed in the blue tissue and

CARE OF CLOTHING

then in brown, nice silk and satin dresses will hold their freshness for a considerable time. This is equally good for laying away soft white flannels. Old blue silk makes as good a wrapper as does the paper.

Woolens and furs can have no better preservative than turpentine and newspaper. There is the advantage with this that if any eggs have been laid in the garments before putting away the turpentine will kill them. Those who insure goods against moths say the insects do not get in after the goods are laid away but the eggs are in them when packed, and that moths lay eggs in articles hung in the open air on the line. Professionals whip furs with tiny, flexible rods and then comb with a fur comb. Thus prepared and rolled in a close cover of newspapers they will keep in any receptacle if turpentine is sprinkled about it. Cayenne is better than any moth-ball except that the wearer of anything thus protected is much inconvenienced on first wearing it after taking from its box. I used it for years and never had a moth touch fur or woolen.

If one has a heavy, expensive overcoat it should be sent to a cleaner before packing away. Perfect cleanliness is one of the best protections from moths, and if a garment has been well cleaned by a professional it is almost certain to come safely through a season even in a house where moths are to be seen at almost any time. By letting the sunshine in all the time the moths will disappear. They are like other evil-doers and have no desire to be in the sunshine or to touch printers' ink.

Haven't you many a time cast away your husband's discarded shirts with a sigh that anything so good should be worthless for any other purpose than for cleaning? Finally I experimented with what I had and first developed an apron.

The shirts were white with a hair line, and good except around the collar. From the back came the front of the apron and the fronts made side gores. A belt and ruffle were found from sleeves and shoulder-piece. The result was a very pretty apron for home wear. This turned out so well that next I made a shirt-waist, which is very easy unless one is larger than her husband. I planned it to use the same buttons and buttonholes, fitting by drawing up on the shoulders. Now all discarded shirts form the basis of rompers or Dutch suits for a three-year-old boy. It is a very simple matter to get either out by laying a pattern on the shirt. This really is a saving worth practising, and the garment can be planned so that the buttons and buttonholes may close the garment. If you do not need to study thrift for yourself, why not do it for some one else who would be glad of your help?

If you have an old carpet that is good except in pattern you can bring it up to date by painting it. Have it perfectly clean and then use a paint that can serve. Any painter can tell you the kind that may be applied, but I may not advertise it. Some paints will fail, but there are several that will turn carpets into quite new articles in appearance. You can turn a rug into oilcloth. Tack it on the floor after it has been washed clean. Cover it with thick cooked paste put on with a brush. Work it well into the rug. When this is dry you must give it two coats of paint and one of varnish. If a border is wanted, use a stencil and another color of paint. For coloring a carpet the paste is not necessary.

CHAPTER XVII
THE FAMILY GARDEN

CHAPTER XVII

THE FAMILY GARDEN

WE know experimentally that the family garden is one of the largest sources of saving of the family income. We started our married life and our garden about the same time, with equal ignorance on both subjects. The garden was established in our back-yard, a plot about 14 x 50 feet in size, of very poor soil where never had garden been. The Man dug it thoroughly, thus cultivating muscles never before much exercised and learning what it means to earn his food by the sweat of his entire body.

The soil was very hard to spade, but was finally dug to a good depth and left to sun and ripen until planting time. As gardening was an experiment, and our dollars were not numerous enough to waste we decided not to buy fertilizer but to enrich our ground with our waste from the table and such wood ashes as we had. Much of the garbage was burned on the inside top of the stove which is a good way to dispose of it and makes no odor if drafts are open. Garbage properly treated in a compost heap becomes good fertilizer but we did not know that then, and there was no place for compost. Not buying fertilizer was a mistaken economy, but nature was very good to us for all that. Some plants are greedy eaters and thrive better for every mouthful of food given them.

One of the encouraging things to the amateur gardener is the will of nature to have things live, and the tenacity of life in the seeds and plants. They will resist lack of proper food and water, but they will not thrive after bugs begin to live on them, and the only plants in our garden that did not have some kind of a bug haunting them were okra and peppers.

Our seeds were given us by a sister whose husband is a champion garden-maker, and there was the expense of thirty-nine cents for a small hand sprayer, which was another mistaken saving. Spraying is so large a part of garden making that it pays to provide one's self with as large a sprayer as one can work. Bordeaux mixture cost seventy-five cents, and we bought tomato plants to the extent of thirty cents, a total cost of one dollar and forty-three cents. The time cost after the seeds were in the ground was about half an hour daily. The average would be higher if digging and planting were included. Most of the work was done early in the morning, and occasionally some little in the evening.

We made the mistake of all beginners and planted enough in that small space to have supplied an acre of ground, and the seeds were so thick together that they had no chance to grow. We planted peas, beans, onions, summer and winter squash, carrots, Swiss chard, spinach, radishes, peppergrass, corn, cucumbers, tomatoes, both seeds and plants, beets, turnips, cabbage, lettuce and okra, these not in rotation but all as nearly at once as we could get them into the ground.

Peppergrass was the first return. It is like watercress and we used it for salad and sandwich filling. There was a second crop of that and we combined with lettuce. We gave away pecks of it, and at the market price of cress it had a money value of a dollar and a half. The peas did not thrive and we had only a quart, worth eight cents; the beans became rusty and we did not get half as many as we should have had, but we sold four quarts at twelve cents each, and canned six quarts. We had ten quarts to eat so our beans brought us two dollars

THE FAMILY GARDEN 283

and forty cents. Of shell-beans there were four quarts, price twenty cents a quart. Onions made sets for the second year, but were worthless to us except for the flavoring value of the tops. There were two quarts of little carrots from thinning the row, and they were delicious but not worth more than six cents. There were sixty large ones, the price of which at that time would have been fifteen cents. The Swiss chard was the most profitable article raised. It furnishes a very delicate greens not often found in the market because it wilts very quickly. We had twenty-six pecks, sold five at forty cents a peck, canned a dozen jars, gave away three pecks, and had it often on the table. At the market price of spinach it brought ten dollars and four cents.

Four plantings of radishes gave us 361 heads or thirty-six bunches at five cents each, total, one dollar and eighty cents;

there were thirty-five cucumbers, valued at one cent each; from the tomatoes we got a peck of ripe ones and four pecks of green ones, the ripe valued at thirty cents, the green at sixty; we had one hundred heads of lettuce from three plantings, and that summer lettuce never went below ten cents. Part of the time the price went to sixteen cents, but we did not sell any of ours and reckoned its value, at the lowest cost, to be ten dollars. There were five summer squashes, worth ten cents, and six winter squashes worth fifty cents.

Three kinds of bugs worked hard all day and night to make a living from the squash and cucumbers and finally destroyed the vines in spite of efforts with the sprayer. The amount destroyed was several times greater than the crop secured. From the beets were gathered twenty-one quarts of tops with the little beets, and five quarts were canned. The

THE FAMILY GARDEN

marketman told me these were worth four cents a quart, total eighty-four cents. Of the roots there were two pecks, worth twenty-five cents; out of all the corn, only one ear grew to maturity, but it was perfect. I sold twenty-five cents' worth of young turnip greens, and three turnips (two cents) were eaten at home. From the green tomatoes six quarts of pickles were made. The okra yielded a pint of so little value it was not counted, and the peppers had no selling value, as they were too small, but they served as seasoning.

There is another side to the story. Not one seed of spinach sprouted; the cabbage label blew off and when the young plants appeared I thought they were weeds and pulled up all but three before the Man told me what they were. These were finally devoured by cabbage-worms. The bugs devoured the squashes and cucumbers, but enough fruit was gathered from them to pay for having planted and tended the seed.

Owing to business necessities we were obliged to move to another city at the end of August and as our garden was late, there was more left in it than we had gathered from it. The bed of chard was still in full bearing, the tomatoes only beginning to ripen, and those from seed planted by us were heavy with green fruit; in the ground ungathered were beets, carrots, turnips, beside chard, tomatoes, lettuce, and peppergrass. In giving prices I have given those common in Baltimore markets that summer, and they are much less than present prices.

It is wonderful how generous Nature is to those who give her a chance, and if she gives thus liberally to two ignorant beginners, what will she not give to those who plant properly, and feed fertilizers with full hand? We might have had twice as much for our work had we not economized at the source of profit. You must remember that every cent paid out that does not bring a return is loss. It was waste to plant twice as much as there was space for, because the plants that grew did not accomplish nearly as much as was natural to them. If one pays a man by the hour or day, from the garden must much more profit be gained.

We made a great profit because we had practically no expense and all that came to us after one dollar and forty-four cents was gain. We sold to persons near by who came for the vegetables that could be bought fresh from the ground. Had we tried to sell, we might have sold much more. Some things we would not sell at all because we wanted all there was. We felt that with $30.14 to our credit our investment paid, and we are enthusiastic advocates of the pleasure and profit in one's own garden. Beside the practical side of abundance of fresh vegetables, there is the delight of seeing things push up their little green heads, put out new leaves, — yes, it surely pays to have a garden. It was not by accident that Eden was a garden.

THE END

Printed in the United States
116417LV00007BA/32/A